Reclaiming Our Teaching Profession

The Power of Educators Learning in Community

Reclaiming Our Teaching Profession

The Power of Educators Learning in Community

Shirley M. Hord
Edward F. Tobia

Foreword by Karen Seashore Louis

Teachers College, Columbia University
New York and London

Published by Teachers College Press, 1234 Amsterdam Avenue, New York, NY 10027

Library of Congress Cataloging-in-Publication Data

Hord, Shirley M.
  Reclaiming our teaching profession : the power of educators learning in community /
    Shirley M. Hord, Edward F. Tobia ; foreword by Karen Seashore Louis.
      p. cm.
  Includes bibliographical references and index.
  ISBN 978-0-8077-5289-0 (pbk. : alk. paper)
    1. Teachers–Professional relationships–United States. 2. Professional learning
  communities–United States. 3. Teachers–In-service training–United States. I. Tobia,
  Edward F. (Edward Francis) II. Title.
  LB1775.2.H675 2012
  370.71'1–dc23   2011031858

ISBN 978-0-8077-5289-0 (paper)

Printed on acid-free paper
Manufactured in the United States of America

19   18   17   16   15   14   13   12   8   7   6   5   4   3   2   1

This book and our thinking has been greatly enhanced by the heroic teachers and principals who took the risk to engage with one another in authentic professional learning communities and who have demonstrated to us how their ongoing learning encounters truly professionalize our profession.

Contents

Foreword

EDUCATORS HAVE BEEN TALKING about the intersection of professional learning, powerful teaching, and better schools for over 30 years. Those conversations have prepared the ground for this book, but it comes at just the right moment. The steam is coming out of simplistic versions of the accountability movement, which assume that setting achievement targets and measuring outcomes will produce systemic change. At the same time, unions and scholars who are concerned with the core of classroom practice are coming around to the idea that old models of professionalism, based largely on rigorously measuring inputs and relying on self-monitoring to ensure quality, are non-starters in today's world. Shirley Hord and Ed Tobia have reached out to help educators find a personal and collective way forward, using their own deep experience as well as other's data to examine where U.S. schools have come from over the last century, what they are like now, and what they can become. The result is a book that is clear in its purpose and its presentation.

Where have we been? Too many books that are written for today's educators assume that the events of a decade ago are deep history, but Hord and Tobia remind their readers that we will have a difficult time preparing for tomorrow if we do not recall the past. The primary audience for this book is people who entered the profession well after the tumult of the 1960s and 1970s, and who did not (as I did) attend the schools of the 1950s, where many classrooms were homogenous and focused on simple basics. In addition, they remind us that there was a time, not very long ago, when preparation standards were lower than today, teachers could expect minimal changes in the content they were expected to teach over their career, professional development barely existed, and teachers were expected to work almost entirely alone and unsupervised. The mental models that developed during that time still shackle today's teachers and administrators, no matter how many times they pronounce the mantra of data-driven decision-making and team learning. Finally, they provide an overview of the movement to professionalize teaching, which began in the 1970s and 1980s. The authors lay out, clearly and unambiguously, what it means to be a professional teacher. While many of the definitions of professionalism focus on the structures that maintain guild exclusivity, the authors move into the heart of professionalism, which they identify as continuous learning and improvement, both around subject matter and instruction. The work of teaching today is fundamentally different than it was when I (and most baby boomers) were in school, and it has changed even more radically when one factors in the increasingly hot policy environment that surrounds schools.

There is, however, an answer beyond the simple demand for teachers to work harder at a more complicated job. The answer lies in reorienting the educational profession's approach to its own learning. The core of the book's argument is best summarized in Chapter 2:

> No longer is it possible for teachers to rely solely on their own personal bank of curriculum and instruction. No longer is it possible to rely on yesterday's classroom practices. There is a clear mandate for educators at all levels to gain the expertise to understand and to use standards in their planning and delivery of instructional practices. . . . there is a clear call for educators to become learners in order to develop appropriate knowledge and skills, to achieve and maintain effectiveness with students.

Assertions like this can be easy, and we see many of them in op-ed pieces and in the more popular professional magazines. It is much harder to put one's finger on what it means. The remaining chapters of the book spell out what needs to happen, how the work of teaching must change to make it happen, and what will make a new model for schools work well for adults, children, and communities.

I was pleased to see that the problem of "professional learning communities" as an administrative "reform du jour" was tackled head-on, because it conforms to my own experiences in talking with teachers. Most teachers today are in a school that has PLCs–at least in name. Many of them have administrative facilitators or data coaches to help them do their joint work. Administrators are enthusiastic, but teachers often view their PLC as "just another meeting" that is a distraction from the real and very difficult work that faces them in their classrooms. "We work collaboratively" is a slightly more enthusiastic response, but may cover up the sharing of practices that do not get at the heart of significant learning, while a response that "we engage in continuous school improvement cycles" may cover up limited learning with a mound of planning and reporting. In sum, what is important is to focus on what is being learned, how it is being applied, and with what effects.

The core of this book's value, however, lies in Hord and Tobia's articulation of a clear, research-based behavioral map of what it means for a teacher to be part of a learning community. The map is a valuable tool that enables self-reflection and collective reflection on whether a "PLC meeting" is actually accomplishing a learning goal. It is worth buying the book for this contribution alone, but the book is also rich with deep and detailed case materials that allow readers to feel the bones of the work of teachers as they elaborate challenging learning tasks for themselves, explain what they have learned to others, look for new ideas and information (both in and outside the group), and develop a long-term agenda to study changes in their practices. In one sense, the cases may remind one of a home-grown version of the Japanese "lesson study" model, but adapted to broader topics and a more extended effort to make fundamental changes in the way in which a student learning problem is approached. In addition, some of the case materials show situations where an issue or problem is identified by an administrator or a specialist, but is spread to create ownership by most teachers. This is an important aspect of the book, because it does not romanticize the professional teacher as operating outside of a system of influence that includes administrators, district office staff, and outside experts. The point is that teachers engage deeply with the new ideas and become active participants in making them meaningful in practice.

Of course the authors acknowledge that this is hard and steady work, and that it requires structures and administrative support if it is to occur. They point, in particular, to the problem of how to create professional learning cultures where they do not already exist. While enabling structures matter (time, space, materials, expertise), the book suggests the importance of creating learning opportunities rather than requiring PLCs. In some of the cases that Hord and Tobia report, early teacher learning opportunities seem weakly connected to critical student outcomes, but effective principals understand that changing ingrained patterns of isolation and individual learning take time and must be built slowly.

If teacher professionalism is all about learning, then learning, according to the authors, is all about developing relationships. Principals can't influence teachers if they are not trusted; teachers won't talk about their practices honestly unless they feel not only safe, but respected by their colleagues. Where districts and schools are at odds, principals and teachers will not be inclined to take the risk of pointing the finger at themselves. By moving back and forth between the importance of structure and purpose, and the reality of how central relationships are to maintaining commitment in the complicated and high pressure environment of today's schools, Hord and Tobia provide a practical, do-able alternative to rapid turnaround that may change test scores but does not provide a sound basis for long-term success.

–Karen Seashore Louis,
Regents Professor of Organizational Leadership Policy and Development,
University of Minnesota

Preface

WELCOME TO OUR LEARNING COMMUNITY, where we will explore the status of education as a profession, the development of a professional consciousness, and the relationship between professionalism and working in a professional learning community (PLC). We will examine the development of professionalism in education, as well as the role that PLCs now command in educators' lives.

Most everyone recognizes that the reason, or the purpose, for which we have schools is *student learning*. They also agree that the factor that is most influential in impacting student learning is *quality teaching*. To increase, expand, or improve quality teaching, *continuous professional learning* is the key. The operative word here is *learning*, and the PLC is learning's most powerful context.

In this book, we hope to provide steps and tools for dedicated educators to develop a truly professional approach to their work through continuous learning and authentic collaboration. The book will address how educators working and learning in community (authentic PLCs) play a significant role in moving from a profession driven by test scores and fear of accountability sanctions to a profession committed to students and dedicated to working and learning together.

The goal of these communities of learners is to increase the knowledge, skills, and capacity of education professionals. When this goal is successful, teachers will be on the pathway to professionalism, and all our students in all our schools will be provided a powerful school experience that results in improved student learning outcomes.

Our intention is to describe the current state of teaching in the United States and how we arrived at our current situation where teachers are being told what to do by so many entities that they're not sure who to listen to. It's hard to feel like and act like a professional when so many people are giving you directives about how to do your job. Once the stage is set, the pathway to professionalism in teaching will be lit by research and current practices that can help teachers take control of their world and work, and reduce the need for multiple levels of supervision to ensure quality. Professional teachers take responsibility for the profession.

Introduction

Here, we state the purpose of this book and how we came to think about professionalism as a topic worthy of exploration. It has not been an easy task to address the issue of the professionalization of the profession, but it is one about which we have a profound concern and regard.

We hope that our words, ideas, thoughts, and frameworks for advancing the profession may stimulate you to consider your own ideas and challenge you to action.

Chapter 1: What Is a Profession? What Does It Mean to Be a Professional?

In this chapter, we lay the groundwork for the readers' understanding of the generic term *professional* as society has come to define it. We do this through reviewing the literature and common practice. We explore whether teaching fits the generally accepted definition of a profession or whether it is, as some have called it, a semi-profession. We also begin to link the concept of professional learning communities to advancing the practice of teaching as a profession. The insights gained from these inquiries provide a base from which to move forward, looking at creating a pathway to professionalism.

Chapter 2: Evolution and Development of the Professional Learning Community

This chapter focuses on the evolution of teaching in the United States and traces the PLC concept from its early inception through its development and focus on continuous adult learning and its relationship to increased student performance.

In the early years of this country, students of all ages and capabilities typically attended school in a one-room schoolhouse with a single teacher serving all. Here, the teacher worked, with little preparation, as well as s/he knew. Even when schools became multiple classroom entities with college-trained teachers frequently using district or other recommended curriculum, the teacher struggled to meet the needs of all students. The publication of Susan

Rosenholz's book (1989) on the impact of teachers' workplace on their perfor-mance revealed how teachers meeting and working together influenced their work and their service for students. At this same general time, Peter Senge's book on the learning organization (1990) lent weight to the productivity of employees coming together to plan and work collaboratively. These publica-tions stimulated researchers to look into this new professional development structure of collaborative learning and its possibilities.

Chapter 3: Influences on the Profession

An array of organizations–their politics and policies–have impacted edu-cators and the expectations for what educators will do, and for the esteem or lack thereof by the public and by the profession itself. We explore the impact that four such influences have had:

- National/state/district policy (e.g., the impact of Sputnik, *A Nation at Risk,* and the No Child Left Behind legislation);
- Teacher and administrator organizations (e.g., American Federation of Teachers, National Education Association);
- Research on professional learning (Darling-Hammond, Wei, Andree, Richardson, & Orphanos, 2009; Joyce & Showers, 2002); and
- Professional organizations (e.g., Learning Forward [formerly National Staff Development Council], Association for Supervision and Curriculum Development, National Commission on Teaching and America's Future, the National Board for Professional Teaching Standards).

These four influences are examined for the challenges they represent as well as their contributions to the current regard in which education is held.

Chapter 4: Beyond the Catchphrase . . .

Like any new idea, strategy, or approach, PLCs have been defined and operationalized in multiple ways by well-meaning practitioners, some of whom are consistently looking for the next new innovation. In these cases we have accessed a great deal of information about what teachers and leaders are doing when they are "doing it." Here, we explore the problems of an "innova-tion du jour" and how becoming a popular idea in education often relegates an effective strategy to the vast graveyard of failed reforms, as Seymour Sara-son suggests in *The Predictable Failure of Educational Reform* (1993).

Although some of these approaches may result in their desired ends, the research has informed us of what effective PLCs look like and how they act. We have cast our "bets" and rested our case on the descriptions of PLCs from this research. These descriptions come from studies whose findings are grounded in robust and rigorous explorations. From these findings, we set forth an operational definition of PLCs, supported by images of what teachers and their administrators do when participating in a PLC and what leaders at the school and district level do to initiate, promote, develop, and support PLCs. These images have been translated into an Innovation Configuration Map. This tool describes precisely what individuals do as they work together in communities of professional learning.

Within the identification of challenges in the previous chapter that inhibit the development of true learning communities, and the promising policies that are beginning to promote the idea, we develop a case for more consistently and intentionally linking continuous adult learning and student learning. This case is grounded in the benefits of effective or high-functioning PLCs to both staff and students. Such benefits include:

- Increased staff learning that accesses deep content knowledge and a repertoire of instructional strategies that result in more effective classroom instruction;
- A shift in thinking, for teachers and administrators, as they become continuous reflective practitioners, always exploring alternatives for increased teaching performance;
- Enhanced, enriched, improved student performance;
- Greater respect, efficacy, and professional identity of the staff members for themselves, their colleagues, and the profession.

Chapter 5: What Educators *Do* in a Professional Learning Community

Three stories of PLCs in action provide a clear picture of the steps taken by three schools as they have developed into communities of professional learners. Even though the path was different for each school, we feel that they each exemplify what individuals actually do when they come together as learners in a community of professionals. The teachers in the three schools are on their way of becoming true professionals who need less direct monitoring to perform their job well. Principals in these schools act more like servant leaders and instructional colleagues than supervisors. Teachers hold one another accountable and take mutual responsibility for all teachers' learning and the learning of all students.

Chapter 6: Turning the Finger Around

Returning to the characteristics of professionals cited in Chapter 1, we celebrate the current attention focused on PLCs and the opportunity this focus provides for the continuous professional learning of all educators. One of the characteristics of a professional person is the continuous study of his/her field's content knowledge and the skills or behaviors expected of professionals in this "line" of work.

In their practice, communities of professional learners express the shift in the culture of their school from isolation to collaborative learning and work. Further, these educators work and learn together to continuously improve their practice, and to add knowledge to the field of education that benefits others—this adds weight to the image of the educational professional. Once this ethic of continuous improvement becomes the norm for teaching, teachers are well-situated to take greater control over the work they do and define the expectations for members of the profession.

Chapter 7: Structures, Schedules, and Other Necessary Stuff: Creating or Reframing Professional Learning Communities

The requirements for launching and developing PLCs—in order to improve the staff's effectiveness and enhance their professional status—begin with logistical/structural factors: time and locations to meet for study and learning; material resources for learning (books, journals, videos, and so forth); and human resources (conference fees, travel funds to visit other schools, fees for consultants and coaches). This chapter focuses on the development and use of organizational structures, protocols, and tools that help teachers remain focused on the real purpose of professional learning communities: improvement of instruction through ongoing reflection on what students need to know and be able to do; best practices for teaching that knowledge; and those skills, assessment of student learning, and the needed modifications when students have not met learning expectations.

Chapter 8: Relationships: The Soul of Professional Learning Communities

Although the structural factors are vital—how can community learning be conducted without the time for staff to convene, without a clear purpose, and without a place to do it—the personal or relational variables are imperative. Supporting the staff in developing high regard, respect, and trust for one another requires modeling, development, and patience. Stories of schools that have been successful in these endeavors provide the reader with real-world examples.

Chapter 9: And Yet . . . Becoming a True Professional

There is the potential that teachers meet in PLCs on a regular basis, have conversations about teaching and learning, use some ideas from those conversations in their classroom practice, and still are not meeting the expectations that are set for the profession. We will recommend a set of steps to be taken to reduce the need for high-stakes evaluation that teachers are currently facing. That degree of supervision has the tendency to de-professionalize teaching by ensuring that teachers follow expectations set by others, not by themselves as professionals.

A substantial amount of time and patience, coupled with persistence, will be required to promote the status of education as a profession. When this goal has been achieved, high regard from the general public will reflect its success. Elevating the teaching profession to the high levels experienced by medicine and law will not be easy (individuals working in medicine and law could not be in that position without a firm grasp of the necessary content and skills, and a commitment to continuously improving the capabilities demanded of those professions), but readers are encouraged to use the ideas and professional tools presented in this book to make the incremental changes in attitude and practice needed to achieve the true professional status of educators.

Introduction

> Classroom teaching . . . is perhaps the most complex, most challenging, and most demanding, subtle, nuanced, and frightening activity that our species has ever invented. The only time a physician could possibly encounter a situation of comparable complexity would be in the emergency room of a hospital during or after a natural disaster.
>
> Lee Shulman, *The Wisdom of Practice* (2004)

AS A PROFESSION, educators have made great progress in the past 30 years. Schools that were never designed to meet the needs of all students are achieving unprecedented results, but the fact remains that we haven't been successful with all students in all our schools. Not only do we lose students at an unacceptable annual rate, but our profession also loses nearly 50% of new hires within the first 5 years of teaching. For the past few years in both casual and formal settings we have talked about how we feel about these dismal statistics, and it infuriates us that we know enough to successfully teach *all* children but, as a profession, we are only doing what we know we could do in a relatively few locations across the country.

In *The Knowing-Doing Gap* (2000), Pfeffer and Sutton suggest that institutions get caught up with gathering information rather than putting it into practical use. They propose that the best way to overcome the knowing-doing gap is to acquire knowledge through doing. When a person is engaged in a learning activity, the mind is already at work thinking of applications for the new learning–anticipating challenges and how to confront those challenges. That kind of learning is in direct contrast to much of the learning in which teachers still engage. They attend a workshop, come back energized with new learning, but rarely apply that new learning systematically or incorporate new behaviors into their repertoire (Darling-Hammond et al., 2009; Joyce & Showers, 2002).

The idea that, as a profession, we thwart the very change we hope to initiate, has been plaguing educators for generations. Many current educators joined the profession to bring about a transformation in society. Those youthful, passionate teachers who experimented with open classrooms, individualized education, and interdisciplinary instruction have aged and been hardened by the political realities of shifting federal and state legislative priorities, school board policies, and the demands of district and school administrators. Many have simply retired, but others have moved into leadership positions that focus more on getting students to achieve on tests than on student learning.

Kegan and Lahey (2001) remind us that there is an aspect of our being that is inclined to prevent change, "despite our best efforts to lead for change, and sometimes even in spite of the sincere intention many of us have to change, very little change actually occurs!" (p. 3). Their book, *How the Way We Talk Can Change the Way We Work*, begins with focusing on our commitment to putting our values into action. If we value being successful with all students in all schools, how do we do the right things—those things we already know to do—so that student learning improves?

All educators have endured traditional education institutions that have focused more on the transmission of knowledge than inquiry, and in this book we would like to do more than transmit additional knowledge. We have engaged in transformational experiences that have led us to believe that learning must be active and is often most effective in community; we hope to use our experiences in professional development to frame a process so that readers can put the information provided in this book into practical use.

Teaching as a Subversive Activity (Postman & Weingartner, 1969) helped move the profession of teaching to a focus more on questions and generating ideas than facts and right answers. This message still speaks to us today. Their book, written over 4 decades ago, and many others since then have opened the door to thinking about the education of our children as much more than the transmittal of facts and patriotic ideals but a wholly human interaction in which the adults carry a moral responsibility to do everything possible to successfully teach all children. In over 75 years of combined experiences in schools, we have encountered teachers and principals who are full-fledged, thriving professionals and we have also encountered the others: others who have entered the profession with passion—a fire for teaching and learning—and have had it systematically extinguished by the bureaucracy that is public education. We need to revisit the question asked by Roland Barth 20 years ago: "Who can do what to provide opportunities for periodic recommitment for those who work in schools so that work will remain a vital profession and not become a tedious job?" (Barth, 1990, p. 166).

There is hope to be found in the words of Margaret Wheatley, who had us consider the implications of her own thinking about learning in community: "It is always like this. Real change begins with the simple act of people talking about what they care about" (2006, p. 22). Parker Palmer's writings have also challenged educators with questions such as "If we have lost the heart to teach, how can we take heart again? How can we remember who we are, for our own sake and the sake of those we serve?" (2007, p. 21).

Taking the time to struggle with the big questions such as "What are the standards to which we hold ourselves as educators?" as well as the daily questions like "How do I know that this lesson was effective?" is what true professionals do on a regular basis.

Although this book will touch briefly on the meaning of the term *professional* in other fields, the main purpose will be to stimulate all educators to consider the attitudes of mind and the behaviors that define a professional approach to their work and to improving their ability to learn how to teach effectively. The National Board for Professional Teaching Standards (NBPTS) has made strides toward defining the attitudes and behaviors of effective teachers. But as a voluntary certification program, the NBPTS is not seen as a requirement by any state thus far. It still hasn't met the challenge set by Albert Shanker (then the president of the American Federation of Teachers) in his 1985 speech to the National Press Club to create a national teacher certification board:

> It would be a group that would spend a period of time studying exactly what a teacher should know before becoming certified and the best way to measure that knowledge. . . . Over a period of time, I would hope the board would eventually be controlled by the profession itself, even if it didn't start completely that way.

For several decades, there has been increasing interest in examining what makes an effective teacher. The No Child Left Behind Act sets out the requirement that all teachers be "highly qualified." Organizations such as the National Council on Teacher Quality have emerged to study, define, and measure teacher effectiveness. In 2009, the Gates Foundation provided funding for nine school districts and one coalition of Charter Management Organizations to transform teacher effectiveness policies and practice. The emphasis of this latest interest in teacher quality comes from outside the profession itself and focuses on teacher preparation, teacher evaluation, and policy development. Although each of these is important, our emphasis is to work on the development of the profession among professionals at the school and classroom level—the locus that is closest to students and student learning.

We have learned a great deal from our work in schools to develop, implement, and study the impact of Professional Learning Communities (PLCs). We worked not only with the principals of the schools but also spent a great deal of time developing the capacity of grade-level leaders who were to be the facilitators of the conversations among teachers. Unfortunately, we often found that after months of teachers meeting together on a regular basis using a structured approach to their conversations, there was very little change in teacher practice. Teachers came to the required meetings but most often were unprepared and had an attitude of "Let's just do this and get it over with so I can go back to my classroom and work." We set out to explore the reasons for this problem.

Consider a group of teachers who are most comfortable creating their individual (and individualistic) lesson plans and are then asked to plan together. There is an immediate sense of vulnerability when they are among their peers and have to expose their knowledge (or lack thereof) of the content standards they teach, how those standards are measured on standardized tests, and what instructional strategies work best to teach those content standards. Teachers risk the judgment of their peers if they are either more knowledgeable than their peers or seem to be lacking some of the knowledge and skills that their peers possess. It takes a great deal of trust for teachers to open up to their peers about what they teach, how they teach, and why they chose that particular instructional strategy.

We realized that it's important not only to look at the actions that lead to more professional behavior, but also the conditions or the context in which teachers are working. In a context of strict accountability systems, high-stakes testing, and teacher evaluation systems based on the results of those tests, teachers are less likely to risk the judgment of others; such a context also discourages the openness and authenticity necessary for deep, professional dialogue. Professionalism requires a trusting environment and, although accountability is important, there must be approaches to teacher development and learning that promote rather than inhibit collaboration.

An excellent resource that helps school leaders, be they administrators or teacher leaders, examine the practices that promote trust is *Trust Matters* by Megan Tschannen-Moran (2004). She defines trust as "one's willingness to be vulnerable to another based on the confidence that the other is benevolent, honest, open, reliable, and competent" (p. 17). She expands on these five facets of trust throughout the remainder of her book. Her main point is that school leaders must model and maintain trusting relationships in all that they do in order to develop a climate within a school where teachers can be vulnerable with one another and open to the kinds of professional conversations that encourage teachers to reflect deeply about their teaching–the mark of a true PLC.

We know as a profession that professional learning must engage teachers in ongoing conversations about teaching and learning that are directly related to their daily work with students, and that lead to improved classroom practices. We must not only provide the structures (time, support, meeting protocols, resources, and so on) but also pay attention to promoting a school culture that encourages teachers to feel safe enough to share their successes and challenges, and open enough to listen to the counsel of others. This provides the basis for their work together to solve the significant problems we face as a profession and will be our focus as we explore the pathway to professionalism.

CHAPTER ONE

What Is a Profession?
What Does It Mean to Be a Professional?

Be the change that you want to see in the world.

Mohandas Gandhi

What kind of educator am I?

> Am I always asking the "why" question, a seeker of new content knowledge that deepens my understanding of concepts and big ideas?
>
> Am I the individual who, in the main, adopts new approaches based on colleagues' reports that their students really enjoyed them?
>
> Am I that consistent person, confident that my methods, time-tested for the last decade, will remain appropriate for the next decade?
>
> Am I an explorer of innovative instructional strategies that will produce critical thinking and problem solving, as well as understanding of concepts and skills?
>
> Am I attached to the belief that my students are the ones responsible for their success?

REFLECTING ON THE PAST FEW DECADES of public education, asking these questions of ourselves and many others caused us to wonder what the answers to these questions said about us as professional educators. Eventually, we began asking bigger questions that led us to wonder if our profession has lost its "professionalism," and if so, does it matter? And if it matters, what can we do about it?

No teachers we know have entered the field for financial rewards. Teaching is an occupation that has long been considered a vocation, a calling. Many individuals possess a real passion for education. Yet, some teachers lose their initial zeal due to their treatment as individuals who need close supervision to be effective. As those disenfranchised teachers spend their days in the company of children, they begin to conduct their jobs by rote, following the steps in a teacher's manual, and not giving deep thought to whether or not students are learning until a test is given. It is no wonder that many students either tune out or turn to other pursuits during the school day. Perhaps the fact that our students hide their cell phones while texting friends says volumes about their reaction to the lack of relevance and stimulating instruction from some teachers who have lost their sense of vocation. There are many inspiring teachers who truly care for their students and their learning, but even they find that their passion and commitment for learning is beginning to wane, as they feel the weight of the system they work in bearing down and asking more of them than ever before—in areas that have little impact on student learning.

Dismay about the current condition of teaching and teachers prompts exploration of these issues:

- How can our system of education support teaching and teachers so that our profession can continue to provide a critical service for our children and ensure a better future for us all?
- What does it take to transform teaching into a true profession?

DEFINITION OF A "PROFESSIONAL"

During a recent gathering of teachers who were asked the question, "What does it mean to be a professional?," answers varied from having a depth of knowledge about one's content field to behaviors such as arriving at school before the students to prepare for the day, or avoiding putting details of your personal life on a social network website. We also heard from teachers that being a professional meant that they continue to learn through taking additional coursework or staying current through reading professional journals.

However, in the educational literature about teaching as a profession, some articles raised the question, "Is teaching a profession?" (Taylor & Runte, 1995). That investigation led inevitably to the broader question, "What is a profession?"

The Collins English Dictionary definition of *profession* offers the following:

1. an occupation requiring special training in the liberal arts or sciences, esp. one of the three learned professions, law, theology, or medicine
2. the body of people in such an occupation
3. the act of professing; avowal; declaration [from Medieval Latin professiō, the taking of vows upon entering a religious order, from Latin: public acknowledgment; see profess]

The concept of *professionalism* is an elusive one. However, a number of sources (Bulger, 1972; Burbules & Densmore, 1991; Larson, 1977) provide some clues to an answer. The earliest professions—medicine, law, and clergy—were defined by a set of characteristics, including:

- Formal preparation for one's chosen field, most often through a university;
- A formal association that holds itself responsible for the quality of services provided by an individual in the profession;
- A regulated certification process tied to some form of entry examination;
- A unique set of skills based on a thorough understanding of the knowledge base generated by members of the profession;
- A service that is both unique and vital to society;
- A strong sense of service to the clients or recipients of the professional service;
- An ethical code that guides the behavior of individuals;
- A high degree of respect from the members of society served by the profession.

Teaching seems to align to some extent with all of these characteristics, save one: respect from society in terms of deference to the expertise of teachers, and remuneration consistent with the perceived importance of the work performed. That lack of deference is in part due to what Dan Lortie (1975) has called "the apprenticeship of observation." Almost everyone in our culture has been exposed to over 13,000 hours of observing teachers at work, and therefore feel that they know what teaching is all about. The same is not true for either medicine or law, professions that often seem inscrutable to most. However, there are other areas in which teachers are not placed at the same level as doctors and lawyers: the extensive preparation and apprenticeship to enter the profession, and a standard, formal association that oversees the quality of services provided to students.

In *Teaching 2030*, Barnett Berry and a group of experienced teacher leaders make a key recommendation for improving teacher quality: Have all prospective teachers engage in an extensive internship both in the community in which they will serve and with a network of expert teachers who can guide their development in a true apprenticeship approach. When this recommendation becomes a regular part of preparation for the teaching field, it will signal a move toward greater professionalism. Until then, teacher preparation remains the role of universities designated as institutions that provide bachelor's degrees and advanced degrees in an area of specialization. Although many university programs provide a rigorous course of study and excellent field experiences, the preparation programs vary in quality and lack a universally accepted approach to the preparation of teachers.

Recent attempts to fill teacher vacancies with alternative certification have provided mixed results. There are many high-quality alternative certification programs but as many, if not more, poorly designed fast tracks to certification. One highly touted program is Teach for America, which selects and trains recent college graduates and has them teach in high-poverty areas in the United States for a 2-year term. While it appears effective as a short-term measure to improve teacher quality, it does not address the long-term needs of a nation to have committed, capable, and professional teachers in every school. It also does not address the need for the kind of preparation and development process for career educators that exists for the medical profession.

Voluntary certification by the National Board for Professional Teaching Standards is a move toward a unified set of certification standards for the profession. However, National Board Certification provides advanced certification and is not designed as entry-level certification for new teachers.

In education, there is no exact equivalent of the American Bar Association or American Medical Association, organizations that set standards and monitor the quality of professional services. That function resides most often with state departments of education and, again, the standards can vary quite a bit from state to state. Additionally, teachers rarely hold one another accountable for providing quality services and many mediocre teachers (or even very poor ones) remain in the classroom, further eroding the respect that good teachers deserve from society.

There are many possible approaches to "fixing" an educational system that has pushed the teaching profession into what some have called a semi-profession (Etzioni, 1969; Zouyu, 2002). The suggestions for improvement include improving teacher preparation programs, strengthening the requirements for teacher certification, improving the structure of teacher compensation, modifying the top-down approach of state departments and district offices, creating more opportunities for teacher empowerment, and shifting the nature of teacher unions (Goldhaber & Hannaway, 2009). Still, having highly educated and highly paid teachers does not mean that teachers who enter the profession will bring themselves wholeheartedly into ensuring that students experience success in school.

In this review of literature on what makes a person a "professional," lists of traits and characteristics of professionalism in general are abundant. However, two major categories of characteristics emerged that merit attention as potential pathways to the professionalization of teaching:

1. Professionals have been engaged in a formal preparation and certification process that meets standards set by the profession itself, and
2. They possess a professional orientation that is exemplified by a commitment to the best interest of those served by the profession.

A FORMAL PREPARATION AND CERTIFICATION PROCESS

We propose an audacious goal for America's future. Within a decade—by the year 2006—we will provide every student in America with what should be his or her educational birthright: access to competent, caring, qualified teaching in schools organized for success. (NCTAF, 1996)

Ever since the report *What Matters Most: Teaching for America's Future* by the National Commission on Teaching and America's Future (NCTAF, 1996) highlighted the centrality of high-quality teaching in any attempt to reform schools, there have been successes in strengthening the preparation and certification requirements for teachers across the United States. At the same time, professional preparation is being undercut by fast-track and "boot camp" preparation. Although there is still much to do to match the preparation requirements of a teacher to those of a physician, the teaching profession is better today than it was even 15 or 20 years ago in most of the United States.

However, teachers' development of the knowledge and skills necessary to perform the work of the profession to a high degree of quality remains a challenge. The challenge involves not only the preparation of an individual to enter the profession, but also the requisite ongoing learning and mentoring for an individual to remain current with the most recent advances in the field that address emerging issues, such as the increasing number of English Language Learners and special education students.

The National Commission on Teaching and America's Future has reviewed teacher preparation programs across the country and discovered that most are still preparing teachers for stand-alone teaching in self-contained classrooms. They are not preparing teachers who are prepared to meet the needs of the students in the schools where they will serve, especially students in urban and rural areas. Too many new teachers leave the profession before they develop the skills they need to be truly effective. They feel isolated from their peers and their voices are often not heard as they introduce new ideas that can potentially transform traditional approaches to pedagogy to bring education in line with rapid advances in technology (NCTAF, 2007).

As a profession, we know so much more about what it takes to educate all students who enter the doors of public schools, but the challenges of changing an institution as formidable as schooling children and young adults make it difficult to actualize what we know is best practice. The words of Ron Edmonds written over 30 years ago still apply:

> We can, whenever and wherever we choose, successfully teach all children whose schooling is of interest to us. We already know more than we need to do that. Whether or not we do it must finally depend on how we feel about the fact that we haven't so far. (1979, p. 23)

As a profession, we need to use the best practices for successfully teaching all children. We need to prepare teachers who are entering the profession to operate in very different ways from how they were taught in schools. Too many new teachers have been "conditioned" in how to teach, over the course of their own 12 years in elementary and secondary schools. The modeling they have experienced in the classrooms in which they have lived for a significant part of their lives is what so many teachers fall back on once they are placed in a classroom (i.e., teacher-centered lecture, or simple question/answer instruction). Many strategies have been used to encourage teachers to move away from these pedantic methods and to adopt instructional strategies that promote greater student engagement and learning. However, across the country, too much instruction is still teacher-led and of a mediocre quality.

The economic downturn of 2010–11 will result in the elimination of many teaching positions. A large percentage of the current teaching force will be retiring within the next 10 years (NCTAF, 2010). The resulting teacher shortage cannot be filled by traditional recruiting strategies, especially if preparation and certification requirements continue to strengthen—which they should. The greater challenge to the teaching profession will be how to retain the large percentage (up to 50% in urban and some rural settings) of teachers who exit the field within the first 5 years of teaching.

A 2007 NCTAF policy brief, *The High Cost of Teacher Turnover*, suggests:

> To close this (teaching) gap, it is time to treat teachers like professionals whose preparation, practice, and career advancement are seamlessly aligned around a cohesive knowledge base that is focused on improved student learning. (NCTAF, 2007, p. 13)

Recruiting and retaining teachers as a goal is not sufficient. Teachers who are retained must be committed to the profession and committed to developing themselves as lifelong learners.

A PROFESSIONAL ORIENTATION

Whether or not teacher preparation includes a formal certification process, more important to the profession is teachers' manifestation of a professional orientation toward their work and how that is related to their likelihood to engage in continuous professional learning in an authentic way.

Preparation and attending staff development training sessions may provide teachers with some useful skills that enhance their work with students. But because the stakes have never been higher in education, these hit-and-miss efforts will not be enough. The demands of legislation that hold students, teachers, principals, and schools to high expectations are great. Beyond preparation and training, these demands require educators committed to the best interest of those served by the profession—the students. For example, teachers acting in a professional manner extend themselves beyond minimum expectations and exhibit an ethical and moral responsibility to do everything in their power to ensure the success of their students. To those teachers, teaching is more than a job; it is a calling. Parker Palmer states it best: "Good teaching cannot be reduced to technique; good teaching comes from the identity and integrity of the teacher" (2007, p. 10).

Teachers who perform their work with a clear sense of identity as professionals and a strong personal standard of integrity are reflective about what they do and are committed to continuous learning as a way to hone their skills. Although numerous examples exist of individual teachers who behave in this professional manner and continuously strive to improve their teaching and students' learning, the expectations set by federal and state accountability systems call for schools to provide a quality education for *all* students, not just those lucky enough to have a teacher with a strong professional orientation. In present-day terms, exhibiting a professional orientation demands acting as a contributing member of a community of professional learners rather than teacher as independent hero.

The Courage to Critique

In its truest sense, maintaining a professional orientation is a courageous act. If a community of professional learners operates together to its fullest, members are open to listening to feedback from their colleagues and growing from what they hear. They hold one another accountable for not only simple acts, such as coming to meetings on time and with all of the materials they need for the conversation to be productive, but also for doing what they said they would do to improve their teaching and students' learning. Holding colleagues accountable is not part of the culture of teaching in most schools, so any attempt to make a shift in that culture will encounter resistance. A solitary teacher acting as a paragon of professionalism can quickly become a pariah due to professional jealousy. Therefore, it is critical that outstanding teachers maintain a sense of integrity and develop trusting relationships as they move into community with other teachers. It takes a great deal of trust to operate in a situation that requires all teachers to rely on one another in order to achieve the intended results: continuous learning and improvement for all.

Trust

Trust is critical to the development of a community of professional learners and the ability to create a trusting climate is yet another hallmark of a professional (Bryk & Schneider, 2002). Holding one another to high standards does not mean that teachers do not take the time to listen when a teacher has had a particularly stressful day and needs to talk about something other than what's on the agenda. Taking the time to listen and care for one another is one of the elements of creating the safe place in which teachers can be truly open to learning from one another.

The same qualities that engender trust are the qualities that help to define a professional. When teachers come together in professional learning teams, they must be honest with one another about student progress (or lack thereof), open enough to receive ideas and feedback from colleagues, competent enough to share worthwhile strategies with team members, and establish ways to access the best practices in their field. Underlying the qualities of honesty and openness is the essential ingredient in a trusting relationship—benevolence. Teachers need to believe that any vulnerability they share will be received by other teachers with an open heart and a real sense of caring about the individual and the work s/he performs.

Commitment

Yet another aspect of a professional orientation is a commitment to the profession itself. Teachers who mechanically follow the directions in a teacher's manual are performing a job as defined by others. Teachers who act professionally have a clear understanding of the expectations for student learning at their grade level or in their subject area, and use what they know about their content, as well as ongoing evidence of student learning, to adjust instruction on a regular basis to meet the needs of students. These teachers regularly scan the professional literature for ways to improve and are eager to share ideas with colleagues. They readily take on roles of mentoring new teachers, engaging in curriculum development projects, and designing effective professional learning experiences with and for other teachers. They attend, preside over, and present at regional and national conferences. Their motivation is not only to improve themselves, but to encourage growth opportunities for all–teachers, students, and the profession.

Teachers who are committed to the profession continuously reflect on their effectiveness as a teacher, especially reflecting on the impact that their teaching has had on student learning.

ADOPTING A PROFESSIONAL APPROACH

While this book attends to the meaning of the term *professional* in general terms, its main purpose will be to stimulate all educators to consider the attitudes of mind and the practical behaviors that define a professional approach to their work.

Driven by legislative mandates and greater demands from parents and community members, school boards and school administrators are constantly looking for the most efficient means (a silver bullet?) to increase student achievement. Too often, that translates to increasing control over what teachers do, rather than examining and reflecting on the evidence about not only how teachers learn and improve, but also what maintains their sense of vocation and their love of teaching.

An article by Suzanne Donovan in *Education Week* (February 11, 2009) states very succinctly the work that lies ahead of us as a profession:

> The infrastructure necessary for this work is not just bricks and mortar, it also is institutional infrastructure. We need a set of school district "field sites" where university researchers, district and school administrators, and classroom teachers can find support for their efforts to work collaboratively to dissect, evaluate, and improve what goes on in classrooms and schools. These sites would play the role that teaching hospitals play in medicine. Continuing improvement in doctors' practice is not produced by federal mandate; it arises from a profession that builds knowledge and then ensures its members are prepared to use that knowledge well. The same must be true for practitioners in education. (p. 25)

Educators can learn a great deal from other professions that provide novices in the field with opportunities to work closely with others who have greater knowledge, skills, and experience. Those professions also have a governing body that not only certifies members of the profession but also provides direction and guidance for all of its members. Although educators may not find it worthwhile to develop the equivalent of the American Medical Association, a starting point for all parties involved in public education is the development of a mindset that is centered on continuous improvement. Developing that mindset begins with teachers having regular conversations about what matters. What will make the most difference is having those conversations translated into learning that transforms into action in the classroom.

We have much to change when the culture in many schools is one of competition rather than collaboration. Too often, teachers have been hesitant to share what Roland Barth (2006) calls "craft knowledge," and therefore teachers "guard their tricks like great magicians" (p. 11). What is needed is an unambiguous picture of collaborative learning that teachers and principals can easily embrace. Educators need a clear vision that supports the idea that change begins with educators talking about what matters, and what matters is that we have evidence beyond standardized test scores that students are learning. This means that we must have a pretty good idea about what we did and how we did it in order to be able to share that knowledge with others and replicate our successes. This is no small task. It takes an organizational culture that is based on trust, leadership that engages in and promotes continuous learning, and teachers who are willing to be vulnerable with one another in their pursuit of excellence.

If we know as a profession that professional learning must engage teachers in ongoing conversations about teaching and learning that are directly related to their daily work with students, we must not only provide the structures (time, support, meeting protocols, resources, and so on) but also pay attention to promoting a school culture that encourages teachers to feel safe enough to share their successes and challenges, and open enough to listen to the counsel of others and work together to solve the significant problems we face as a profession. Consider the words of Linda Darling-Hammond and colleagues:

> When schools are strategic in creating time and productive working relationships within academic departments or grade levels, across them, or among teachers school-wide, the benefits can include greater consistency in instruction, more willingness to share practices and to try new ways of teaching, and more success in solving problems of practice. (2009, p. 11)

It is in solving the problems of practice that teachers have the opportunity to demonstrate to administrators and legislators that they are ready and willing to be treated as professionals and reclaim the ideals of this truly noble profession.

Recently we noticed a few billboards on major highways in a large metropolitan area that read:

Want to Teach?
When can you start?

The only other such billboards for other occupations that we can recall seeing are those that encourage people driving down a highway to become truck drivers. This imposing sign implies that the only qualification to be a teacher is a desire to teach. It paints a disheartening picture of a profession that requires strong content knowledge, considerable pedagogical and relational skill, as well as patience and tenacity. In an era of strong accountability, mandated curricula, and externally imposed implicit competition among teachers based on merit pay, a professional stance takes on greater urgency. If teachers ever wish to gain the respect given to doctors, they must take on a professional orientation to their work, project an image of dedication and service, hold one another accountable for their own growth and improvement, and take on a shared responsibility for the learning of all students. The pathway to this professionalism lies in teachers engaging in professional learning communities.

CHAPTER TWO

Evolution and Development of the Professional Learning Community

> Teachers in a learning community . . . engage in continuous inquiry about teaching. They are researchers, students of teaching, who observe others teach, have others observe them, talk about teaching, and help other teachers. In short, they are professionals.
>
> Roland Barth, *Improving Schools from Within* (1990)

REVIEWING EDUCATORS' ACTIVITIES, as they existed in early colonial days and thence forward, provides the groundwork for understanding how teachers' and campus administrators' roles have evolved. These roots also help in understanding educators' status as professionals, and how the professional learning community concept has developed.

EARLY TIMES

From single operators to members of a collaborating team, the roles of teachers and their school administrators have changed.

Isolated Entrepreneurs

In the early years of our country, public education was born during the time of the Revolutionary War, when Thomas Jefferson proposed a law for universal education in Virginia. However, at this time in the 18th century, teaching was a home-based activity. Mothers, especially those committed to strong religious beliefs, dedicated time around the fire in the evenings to teach their children to read and to "do their numbers." The Bible was the major, and frequently the only, material available for teaching reading. A slate board accompanied by charcoal from under the kettle of soup, simmering on its hook mounted in the kitchen fireplace, served as teaching equipment for learning to do mathematical calculations.

In these early times, "dame schools" (Monaghan, 1988; Sugg, 1978) developed, making educational opportunities a trifle more available and formalized. The student clientele expanded to children living in close proximity, who were taught by a woman in her home, still maintaining the model of sole educator.

As colonies of settlers were established—homes built, farms created, communities organized, single-owner businesses established—attention turned to the design and creation of churches and the one-room schoolhouse, in the 19th century. Here, a teacher was employed to take responsibility for advancing the wide-ranging capacities and abilities of the students who appeared at the door. The teacher, with little preparation (graduation from primary school; Neil, 1986), continued in solitary isolation as the educator, although older children were frequently called upon to teach the younger.

Certainly, there were no managers or administrators, and the teacher cleaned the furnace, swept the floors, and cared for the facility. Nonetheless, because few individuals in the communities could read or write, the teacher was given high esteem and regard for his/her skills, talents, and perceived wisdom—a high status symbol in the community.

In the 20th century, as schools grew larger, school principals and district superintendents became important for the role they could play in managing the school campuses and the district to which they were assigned. These players on the educational stage enacted their roles in the interest of efficiency, adopted from the business models of the time. Even so, teachers and principals remained isolated, housed in what were "amusingly" characterized as egg crate schools, where they had no substantive communication with other adults about their teaching and management practices.

These cell-like classrooms and cultures promoted insulation from any new ideas, leaving principals and classroom teachers generally as self-employed individuals. Here, individual teachers in their isolated classrooms (even if they shared a classroom wall), conducted their work as best they could, dependent on their personal knowledge of curriculum and instruction, and theory of student learning. Although many schools remain in this pattern, a new model was reported in the late 1900s.

Partnering Colleagues

The 1970s brought team teaching, open classrooms, and increased teacher interaction. Teachers consulted about various students; planned for their daily, weekly, and 6-week units of instruction; arranged for acquisition of materials and equipment for their lessons; and promoted more efficiency in their work. The study of these activities resulted in new insights about the effects of workplace on teachers' morale, knowledge and skills, and other factors (Rosenholtz, 1989).

This shift in the glacier of teacher isolation and the fracture of the physical obstacles to teacher interaction supported the idea of teachers convening together to share their work. There were many teachers who did not welcome this new procedure, but for many it increased their morale and motivation, as well as some innovation. They were not alone in their work, but had colleagues. Although few administrators knew or gave abundant attention to what the teachers were doing when they were meeting, efforts across the nation focused on making these meetings possible. Many schools in many school districts, some with great difficulty, schedule grade-level and department meetings for elementary and secondary teachers. The simple reality of having such time to meet has led to the notion, in the minds of many school administrators, that their school is a PLC.

These new structures and schedules provide time for teachers and principals to meet, but all too frequently the focus is on management. Such management items could include ordering textbooks and other instructional supplies and determining who will have responsibility for ensuring that this is accomplished, scheduling study trips off the school campus, aligning classroom schedules to take advantage of guest speakers, and other activities. In addition, time is frequently allocated for reporting about conferences attended by a team member, or about an instructional activity a team member used that students enjoyed or found appealing. Too infrequently is explicit attention given to articulating the significance or effect of such information, or transferring such new ideas into classroom practices. This pattern of organizing and sharing is what many systems use currently to describe the purpose of their schools' professional learning communities.

Collaborative Workers

Reporting their successes and failures in their meetings with colleagues, teachers began sharing repertoire and working together on various instructional strategies, programs, and projects. Meeting together and creating projects was viewed as valuable, thus teachers were encouraged to work collaboratively. Teachers working together served as a bridge to the possibility of their participation in professional learning communities. In their early genesis and introduction into schools, professional learning communities were described as settings and opportunities for teachers and their principals to work collaboratively.

Campus principals, in general, remained as independent managers of facilities and of people. Their isolation continued, with little or no interaction or sharing with others in their role.

PROFESSIONAL LEARNING FOR EDUCATORS

There were no opportunities for teachers in the early years of this country to engage in teacher education activities focused on learning about how to teach, and to teach effectively. At the outset of the 1800s, graduation from elementary school constituted preparation for teaching (Neil, 1986). The idea of training to prepare for teaching was very slow to develop until the period of 1850–1920, when normal schools provided this service. However, these preparation institutions were deemed to be very uneven in quality and *in-service education* was given more attention in order to address this concern (Neil, 1986). A deficit model of teacher preparation was the approach, which remains prevalent today, although a developmental model is much touted.

The 1970s brought the understanding that teachers were individuals and had differentiated needs. *Staff development* was tagged as offering continuous learning, growth, and change (Alkin, 1992). This in-service period followed the pre-service period, suggesting that teachers should be supported in continuous learning and improvement throughout their careers. As a consequence, in-service days were mandated beginning in the late 1960s, the position of director of in-service education was created, and in-service requirements for districts and states were formalized. Little attention was given to the relationship between in-service education and student learning. However, "we had in-service days, in-service experiences, in-service speakers, in-service requirements, in-service points . . ." (Hirsh & Hord, 2008, p. 337).

The perfect workshop was the target in the 1970s and 1980s. A consuming role of school district staff developers was to find and hire, or to create, in-service opportunities that warranted a value of 5 on a 5-point scale of satisfaction by the participants. Voluminous catalogs touting workshops of every hue and cry, content and process, grade level and academic subject area, were produced in many school districts. Guest speakers and their topics were the order of the day. Such activities typically were located "downtown," away from interaction with teaching colleagues and the teaching environment.

Only later would the teaching staff and building administrators come together to learn the same material, and to discuss how they might apply it to their own teaching and subsequently, to students' learning needs.

In the mid-1970s, the National Staff Development Council (NSDC) was conceptualized and born. The NSDC and its initial few members were all about understanding and articulating the purpose of professional development (note–the label has changed again, from staff development–*in-service* is a dead word, except in uninitiated quarters). The effort was to help constituents across the spectrum to a new view of professional development, that it is more than exposing teachers and principals to new ideas in education.

With the announcements of new standards for teaching and learning in the late 1980s, school districts gave the nod to professional developers, looking to them to be certain that teachers and principals were fully prepared to ensure that all students were successful learners. Programs, institutes, and academies were designed to increase administrator and teacher effectiveness.

Assuming that professional development "had arrived," attention focused on evaluating the impact of professional development. Simultaneously, the federal government announced a national award to recognize school systems that employed professional development that could be correlated to student achievement. In addition, in the 1990s, educational organizations across the nation joined in a process that resulted in the articulation of standards for staff development (National Staff Development Council, 2001). These standards are under further revision to ensure currency.

This process supported the national conversation regarding effective professional development and its contribution to improved educational practice, and the status of educators as professionals. These 2001 NSDC standards can be found in more than 40 states that have adopted the standards into policies and law. And yet, there is a long road to travel to find the standards in everyday practice and to find effective staff development being conducted regularly in our schools and districts. As Schmoker (2003) notes, "It is time to close the gap between what we know and do to promote learning. It is still the rare school that recognizes that teachers, working together, have the capacity–right now–to improve instruction" (p. 39).

DEVELOPMENT OF PROFESSIONAL LEARNING COMMUNITIES

Equating collaborative work with professional learning community remains a current theme, popularly held by many educators and their systems. Working collaboratively is, indeed, a part of professional learning communities, but it is one rib; it is not the whole umbrella. Contributing to the rhetoric of professional learning and its increased power when conducted with groups of educators in community settings, along came standards for the academic disciplines–and a shift in educational policy, and, subsequently, the articulation of sharper and clearer expectations for educational practice.

Learning Educators

Academic subject-matter associations (mathematics, literacy, and science, for example) and state departments of education across the nation developed standards for what students at each level of their educational experience should be able to know and to do. They identified what students are expected to achieve, and, significantly, what educators are responsible to teach so that students learn and actually achieve the standards in a high-quality way.

No longer is it possible for teachers to rely solely on their own personal bank of curriculum and instruction. No longer is it possible to rely on yesterday's classroom practices. There is a clear mandate for educators at all levels to gain the expertise to understand and to use standards in their planning and delivery of instructional practices. There is, consequently, a strong need for supporting teachers and campus administrators with intentional learning, vis-à-vis the standards, and more innovative schooling practices for achieving the standards–to prepare them for enabling students to reach high standards of learning. Thus, there is a clear call for educators to become learners in order to develop appropriate knowledge and skills, to achieve and maintain effectiveness with students.

Many of today's schools are experiencing significant demographic changes in their student population, and are expected to be successful with a diverse population of students. This requires administrators to support teachers in acquiring a broad spectrum of curriculum content, instructional strategies, and appropriate approaches that fit individual students' learning styles. One size does not fit all. Fortunately, there is a broad base of research and exemplary practice that informs administrators and teachers about effective ways to develop students into successful readers, mathematicians, writers, and scientists. To make this a reality, adults learn more powerful ways of operating in their schools and classrooms–*educators are the first learners.*

Professional Learners: Learning Professionals

In these communities of professional learners, it would seem that the three words should be self-evident (Hord & Hirsh, 2008). This means that *the professionals* in a school are those individuals who have the responsibility and accountability to deliver an effective instructional program to students (or the clients of other organizations); in schools, they ensure that students achieve at high levels of learning; these professionals in a school include the teachers, administrators, counselors, media specialists, and others;

they come together as a group, in *community*, where structures and schedules support their meeting; and

whose purpose is to *learn*; improving an entire staff rather than a selected few teachers so that all students gain the benefits of high-quality teaching and achieve successful learning.

It appears that, in a large way, the emphasis in many quarters has been on community–that is, meeting together without consideration of an agenda. This is understandable, given that the teaching staff has historically been very isolated, so that the opportunity to meet is the initial innovation. Another large population of professional learning community advocates suggests and emphasizes the collaboration and collaborative work of the community, rather than that of learning. Indeed, some learning by the participants could result from the collaborative work–as a by-product. But does this learning prepare participants for teaching their 5th-grade students long division tomorrow?

Thus, a major point is, *What* is the focus of the professionals' learning?

Members of effective professional learning communities focus attention on themselves: to acquire specific new content knowledge, new skills, processes, and approaches. They deliberately and intentionally determine their target(s) for their own adult learning, e.g., studying and learning to use "The ABC Writing Program."

A second question is, *Why* are they learning that?

The PLC members explore multiple sources of student outcome data to identify areas of students' successful learning and to celebrate those areas. Subsequently, they re-examine these data to identify areas where students were not successful. The members use these data and their interpretation of them to focus thorough study to determine the root causes of the students' lack of success. They then use these insights as the basis for determining their own learning needs, in order to change their instructional practice to meet the needs of their students. Student needs direct their attention to their own learning.

So, *How* are they doing this learning?

The community of professional learners will explore, discuss, and determine their solutions for poor student performance (in one example, the poor writing performance of their students), and they will also decide how they will learn to use their identified solution—the new program, process, and/or practices. In this story that happened in an elementary school in the panhandle of Texas, the professional learning community members judged that they could purchase a new program, and together study it chapter by chapter. After concluding a chapter, followed by rich discussion of pertinent content and strategies that they would implement in their own teaching practices, they developed lesson plans that each member used in his/her classroom.

At their next meeting, they debriefed, reporting their successes and failures (evidence of student learning), reviewed their understanding of the concepts and procedures, and revised their instructional plan. The new plan was used, debated and debriefed, and revised in several cycles until the members were satisfied that they had gained deep content knowledge and a variety of effective instructional strategies for achieving student learning. Then they moved to the next chapter for their continuous learning agenda.

This brief story of one learning community of professionals should make clear that their meetings are not just a place where they get together regularly. Nor is it a staff group coming together just to work collaboratively. The group cited above has developed into a maturing group of professionals who organize themselves and engage in purposeful, collegial learning. This learning is intentional and its purpose is to improve staff effectiveness so all students learn successfully to high standards.

Attributes of Professional Learning Communities

In school improvement and reform work, staff at the Southwest Educational Development Laboratory in Austin, Texas, reviewed the knowledge base on effective professional learning communities and visited schools where PLC was reported to exist. These activities resulted in staff identifying descriptors of these entities that were successful—that is, where staff were continuously learning, and using this learning in their classrooms to impact student results. At that time, five dimensions or characteristics were noted (Hord, 2004):

Supportive and shared leadership requires the collegial and facilitative participation of the principal who shares leadership—and thus, power and authority—by inviting staff input and action in decision-making.

Shared values and vision include an unwavering commitment to student learning that is consistently articulated and referenced in the staff's work.

Intentional (this term was added subsequent to Hord's 2004 publication) *collective learning and application of learning* requires that school staff at all levels are engaged in processes that collectively seek new knowledge among staff and application of the learning to solutions that address students' needs.

Supportive conditions include physical (structural) conditions and human capacities that encourage and sustain a collegial atmosphere for collective learning (this dimension was subsequently divided into two dimensions—structural and collegial/relational, see Chapter 4).

Shared practice involves the review of a teacher's behavior by colleagues and includes feedback and assistance to support individual and community improvement.

These dimensions are interactive and influence one another, so that it is difficult to consider any one of them in isolation from the others.

Synthesizing findings of ten American studies and one in England, Vescio, Ross, and Adams (2008) report the results of professional learning community impact on classroom practice and student learning. These authors maintain that "At its core, the concept of a PLC rests on the premise of improving student learning by improving teaching practice" (Vescio, Ross, & Adams, 2008, p. 82). These authors concluded that the practices of PLC teachers in the studies changed, albeit in various ways. The practices of the participants became more student-centered over time. Flexibility of classroom arrangements and changes in the pace of instruction to accommodate for differences in students' mastery are additional examples.

In terms of the impact of teachers' participation in PLC on increases in student achievement, eight of the studies provided data that student learning improved. Results of student achievement varied with the strength of the PLC in the school. Although these studies were few in number, their results support the contention that student learning increases when teachers participate in PLCs.

In more recent empirical research (Ermeling, 2010; Gallimore, Ermeling, Saunders, & Goldenberg, 2009; Saunders, Goldenberg, & Gallimore, 2009), a 5-year longitudinal study revealed five keys to creating effective high school (as well as elementary school teacher) learning teams. These findings, reported in *Education Week* (Gallimore & Ermeling, 2010), identify the following five critical factors:

Structure–job-alike teams of five to seven teachers who teach the same course, subject, or grade level, with common teaching responsibilities

Materials–protocols that support the teachers' improvement efforts, with regular opportunities for teachers to share repertoire

Facilitators–peers who assist and guide their colleagues, who model, explain, and encourage the adoption and implementation of new practices

Environments–settings that are stable and dedicated to improving instruction and learning

Stick-to-itness–participants who persevere until there is evidence of increases in student performance

These researchers identified additional contextual factors that play a significant role. Organizational capacity and stable campus leadership that made instructional goals a priority are critical contributors.

Outcomes of PLC for Staff and Students

Benefits of the PLC accrue to both the staff and to students.

Students. In an early study conducted by Lee, Smith, and Croninger (1995), staff worked together to provide high intellectual learning tasks for 11,000 students in 820 high schools characterized as PLC. These students achieved higher academic gains in math, science, history, and reading than those students in traditional non-PLC schools. In addition, students from different socioeconomic family backgrounds produced smaller achievement gaps, students learned more, and learning was distributed more equitably, most notably in the smaller high schools. These outcomes gained the attention of educators.

Staff. In these schools, teachers viewed themselves as responsible and accountable for the development of all students, sharing a responsibility for all students' learning outcomes. (Does this sound like a group of professionals in action?) The faculty and staff expressed more satisfaction and higher morale–they had colleagues with whom to work and share teaching challenges.

A strong positive relationship was found between teachers' professional commitment (found in the professional culture of the schools–again, are these our educational professionals?) and students' performance. After controlling statistically for the effects of poverty, a study in 2002 (Bobbett, Ellett, Teddlie,

Olivier, & Rugutt) found that teachers' professional commitment and collegial teaching and learning in the school culture accounted for 23% of the variation among study schools in school effectiveness and student outcomes on school test scores.

In the university setting, Gonzalez, Resta, and De Hoyos (2005) studied the implementation of policy initiatives to transform the teaching-learning process in classrooms. This transformative approach to classroom instruction was supported by several years of staff development to enable the faculty to change their classroom practices and to develop professional learning communities as a support structure. The results revealed that concerns expressed by faculty, who perceived they were part of a PLC, focused on their own impact on their students. Significantly, those faculty who did not consider themselves members of a PLC expressed concerns about managing their classrooms: time and other logistical management issues, concerns more peripheral to learning. PLC members who were focused on and committed to student gains appear to be the educators who become our professionals.

A note here about the relationship between school improvement and adult learning should be useful. Currently, and for multiple years, the public and the profession have been attentive to the imperative for schools to improve and become more effective so that all students learn well. Those school improvers who have been accepting these challenges know all too well that *improvement* in schools is dependent on identifying what is not working productively and *changing* to a new way of operating. As one wag has suggested, "If you keep on doing what you've been doing, you will keep on getting the same results." Most certainly, we all want new results! Therefore, change(s) must be adopted, followed by *learning* what the change is and how to use it. Efficiently, it could be said that "Change is learning; it's as simple and complicated as that" and this is the first principle advocated by Hall and Hord (2011, Chapter 1, p. 6) in their latest volume on the change process.

The professional learning community serves to promote teachers' continuous learning, and thus, quality teaching, the prime factor in whether students learn well. It also provides the environment wherein teachers inquire into their practices, determine their own learning needs, and increase the potential of developing a professional mindset and demeanor.

CHAPTER THREE

Influences on the Profession

Our schools will not improve if elected officials intrude into pedagogical territory and make decisions that properly should be made by professional educators. Congress and state legislatures should not tell teachers how to teach, any more than they should tell surgeons how to perform operations.

Diane Ravitch (2010a)

WHILE THE FEDERAL ROLE in public education has increased through strict accountability measures (NCLB) and incentives tied to changes in policy (Race to the Top), and some state school boards have taken on the role of curriculum developers (Texas in particular), teachers are doing their best not only to meet the needs of their students but also to respond to the clamoring of the voices they hear most often: administrators trying to meet state and federal mandates, and parents wanting their children to have a successful learning experience. In late 2010, the documentary *Waiting for "Superman"* and the related series of events sponsored by NBCTV and archived as "Education Nation" have stimulated conversations about what has caused the United States to lose its standing as a leader in educational outcomes among industrialized nations.

On the other hand, there are positive influences and emerging movements, among them the increasing attention on professional learning communities, that can counter the negative view held by many about schooling in America.

BARRIERS

Once again, a brief historical perspective helps to demonstrate how the profession has been molded by external influences.

Federal and State Policy

World War II effectively ended the isolationism that had dominated the early years of the United States, and with the launch of Sputnik in 1957, the government in the form of the National Defense Education Act became a significant player in the field of education to elevate our country's ability to compete on an international playing field. In 1965, President Johnson's War on Poverty refocused attention on national rather than international issues and the Elementary and Secondary Education Act was passed to level the playing field for low-income students. Those two events triggered a wave of innovative curricula and instructional approaches that were often poorly implemented and began decades of efforts by external agencies to improve teaching and learning. The "Nation at Risk" report of 1985 added fuel to the fire and started a flurry of additional reform efforts focusing on increased accountability, stronger teacher evaluation processes, and more attempts to improve teachers' work in the classroom through mandated initiatives and an increasing emphasis on developing competition for public schools through school choice, voucher systems, and charter schools. All of the external forces targeted on improving public education merged in the passage of the No Child Left Behind Act of 2001 (NCLB). Although it is often vilified, there is no doubt that NCLB has resulted in higher standards for student learning and increased accountability for some schools that have historically provided students a mediocre education at best and a damaging school experience at worst.

Recent federal policy has targeted the area that has the greatest impact on student learning–teacher quality. That focus has generated a debate between those who feel that teachers must be adequately prepared through a rigorous university program that grants certification (Darling-Hammond & Sykes, 2003; National Council for Accreditation of Teacher Education, 2010) and those who believe that the current certification process is inadequate and must be supplemented (perhaps even supplanted) by a process that allows bright, capable college graduates an alternative pathway to certification (Podgursky, 2004). We do not wish to engage in the debate over teacher certification. However, our inclination is toward a rigorous preparation period for teachers that includes a strong foundation in scientifically based research and an internship period during which beginning teachers engage with more able and experienced peers and develop a culture of collaboration where novice and experienced teachers can learn and improve together.

Federal and state policies nominally support teacher collaboration and professional development; however, they also tend to mandate that teachers engage in activities and behaviors that should be part of what teachers do as professionals. In too many reform agendas, the voice of the teaching profession has been lost. Teachers have been treated, not as professionals but as workers who need to be told what to teach and how to teach it, and be tightly supervised to see that they do what they've been told. As early as 1988, Linda Darling-Hammond clearly identified the issue:

> The basic reason, though, for these top down and increasingly prescriptive approaches is that policy makers do not trust teachers to make responsible, educationally appropriate judgments. They do not view teachers as uniformly capable, and they are suspicious about the adequacy of teacher preparation and supervision. (p. 64)

The well-intentioned federal mandates for a quality education for all have put state departments of education and school administrators in control of the decisions that could and should be made by teachers who, acting as true professionals, can organize learning experiences for students to reach the high standards set by the profession, rather than by legislators or administrators. Teacher's unions have attempted to bring teacher voice back into the decisions being made for teachers about what and how to teach, but their message gets lost among the stories of unions protecting teachers who would be fired if schools had more flexibility. That leads us to discuss what some people have felt is one of the greatest barriers to teachers' professionalism, the persistence of a union mentality that was more suited to the 19th and 20th centuries than the 21st century.

Unionism

Teachers have been seeking a stronger voice in the profession since the earliest days of education in America. As teaching became a mostly female occupation through the 19th century, issues of fair pay for teachers and fairness in hiring became increasingly important. It was not unusual for female teachers to be dismissed for getting married or becoming pregnant, and compensation for teachers has never been at a level comparable to other white-collar professions. During the early years of the National Education Association, the first teacher's union was established in 1857. The union was dominated by men who represented school administrators and college professors. Again, the voice of teachers was lost and they (mostly women) were seen as needing guidance and supervision. While the mantra for the unions has been the professionalization of teaching, emphasis on fairness for all has reduced the argument into one that focuses more on teacher rights than on teacher responsibilities.

Teacher's unions are maligned in the eyes of the public by books such as *The Teacher Unions: How the NEA and AFT Sabotage Reform and Hold Students, Parents, Teachers, and Taxpayers Hostage to Bureaucracy* (Lieberman, 1997) and *The War Against Hope: How Teachers' Unions Hurt Children, Hinder Teachers, and Endanger Public Education* (Paige, 2007). Movies like *Waiting for "Superman"* (2010), described by Diane Ravitch (2010b) as propagandistic, and stories in the press about how unions prevent schools from setting high expectations for teachers send the message that unions are at fault for low test scores, high dropout rates, and an overall lack of professionalism among teachers. Although there is evidence that some union officials have engaged in tactics unbecoming to an occupation that considers itself a professional career, there is still reason for teachers to come together in defense of their professionalism. In Texas in the mid-1980s, Ross Perot backed a legislative mandate that required all teachers to take a basic literacy test. Teachers balked, but they did what they were told and took the test. Unions exist in Texas, but as a "right to work" state, teachers are free to choose to belong to a union or not, which critics of "right to work" laws see as limiting the influence that unions have. As a result, unions made strong statements against the literacy test, arguing that state legislators should also be required to take the test. In the end, teachers took the test and legislators did not, further eroding the public's view of teaching as a true profession.

When *Time* author Joe Klein (2011) interviewed a striking teacher in Wisconsin, they engaged in one of the long-debated issues in education—who determines teacher quality. The context for that discussion was the flashpoint topic of laying off teachers based on the union stance of "last hired, first fired" versus Klein's assertion that those dismissed during an economic downturn should be teachers who did not perform well. The union contention is that principals are not able to equitably determine the quality of one teacher over another. Klein described the union stance with these cutting words: "They lashed themselves to strict seniority rules more appropriate to assembly-line workers than would-be professionals." This encounter between a newsman and a teacher raises the question of how teachers might shift the mindset of the public about their status as "would-be professionals." One step toward developing a culture within schools where teachers hold one another accountable for their performance in the classroom and success with students is to create the structural and relational conditions in which teachers work, plan, analyze, and learn from one another. That culture of collaboration and interdependence encourages teachers to "step up" and show their colors as true professionals.

There is certainly a need for the teaching profession to work as a collective to protect teachers from arbitrary acts and expectations to work extended hours under a compensation system that doesn't encourage them to go above and beyond. There are a few positive examples of unions that have gone beyond the traditional union stance and have focused more on improving teaching as a profession (Toledo, Ohio, and Rochester, New York, come to mind). When former Washington, DC, school district chancellor Michelle Rhee tried to pay teachers a professional salary and then hold high expectations for their performance, the union initially went along with the proposal (the agreement fell apart when she left). However, the few examples of teachers behaving badly (for example, poor performing teachers, supported by unions, being shifted from one school to another in "the dance of the lemons") effectively destroy innovative and positive ideas, resulting in the general opinion that teachers are not professionals who deserve additional compensation. An effective way that teachers can convince the public how professional they can be is to engage with one another as partners in learning how to improve instruction in ways that improve student learning–i.e., by participating as members of a professional learning community.

BOOSTERS

If the teaching profession is ever to gain the respect it deserves, there must be countervailing forces to the perception that public education in general and teachers in particular are in need of fixing.

Research About Professional Learning Communities

> Research has steadily converged on the importance of strong teacher learning communities for teacher growth and commitment. . . . Schools whose staff members espouse a shared responsibility for student learning and are organized to sustain a focus on instructional improvement are more likely to yield higher levels of student learning. (Judith Warren Little, 2006)

The research about the positive impact of professional learning communities has come from a variety of sources. As early as 1982, Judith Warren Little was investigating the impact of collegiality (as opposed to teachers working in isolation) on student achievement. Rosenholtz (1989) found that schools exhibiting higher levels of collaboration and professional sharing were more likely to have higher levels of student achievement. Hord and colleagues (2004) were beginning a study of communities of continuous inquiry and improvement in the early 1990s and studies by McLaughlin and Talbert (1993), Louis , Kruse, and Associates (1995), and Newmann and Wehlage (1997) supported the concept that teachers acting in collaborative groups were most effective when they not only planned together but also learned together. It's important to note that it is not simply cooperation among teachers that makes the greatest difference, but it is teachers who take collective responsibility for student learning (Lee, Smith, & Croninger, 1995).

More recently, two separate teams of researchers (Gallimore, Ermeling, Saunders, & Goldenberg, 2009; Vescio, Ross, & Adams, 2008) have found that when teachers were involved in professional learning teams, their behaviors changed in ways that characterize professional behavior: Their collaborative work focused on solving significant problems they faced with instruction and student learning and they were more likely to seek the skills and knowledge they needed.

Even though the research is compelling, many teachers across the country still operate in isolation or they may do some planning together but their conversations don't move beyond superficial sharing to developing the deep learning that comes from engaging in authentic professional learning communities. As all teachers embrace an ethic of ongoing learning and development, the obstructions in the pathway toward being seen, treated, and compensated as professionals are cleared.

Teachers who act in a professional manner engage in some activities that have not been typical in many schools. They:

- Come together not only to plan but also to reflect on the impact of their teaching on student learning and either share ideas about needed instructional adjustments or seek additional learning to help them meet the learning needs of students;
- Hold one another accountable for engaging in the reflection and learning necessary to improve instruction and student learning;
- Share the responsibility for student learning of all students touched by the professional learning team;
- Not only readily open their classrooms to instructional leaders and fellow teachers, but also actively seek feedback about the effectiveness of their teaching.

Professional Organizations and Publications

Much of what we have learned about professional learning communities is summarized in the key findings of a status report on professional development. Linda Darling-Hammond and colleagues (2009) state that:

> Professional learning can have a powerful effect on teacher skills and knowledge and on student learning if it is sustained over time, focused on important content, and embedded in the work of professional learning communities that support ongoing improvements in teachers' practice. When well-designed, these opportunities help teachers master content, hone teaching skills, evaluate their own and their students' performance, and address changes needed in teaching and learning in their schools. (p. 7)

The report was commissioned by the National Staff Development Council (NSDC, now called "Learning Forward") as one of three such reports on the condition of professional learning in the United States. Although the report acknowledges that most teachers in the country do not experience opportunities for high-quality professional learning, it does provide support for NSDC's purpose: "Every educator engages in effective professional learning every day so every student achieves."

That sentiment is echoed in numerous websites and publications (electronic and hard copy magazines) such as *Educational Leadership*, produced by the ASCD; www.teacherleaders.org, the website of the Teacher Leaders Network; and others too numerous to list. The bottom line is that more and more anecdotal evidence and research is accumulating that concludes teachers engaging in authentic professional learning teams results in improvements in teaching and learning.

This idea brings us back to the point that although there are many influences thwarting or encouraging teachers to act more professionally, it is the very practice of behaving as a professional, engaging in the practice of professional learning communities, that will open the pathway for teachers to be seen as true professionals. In *Educational Professionalism: An Inside-Out View*, Glazer (2008) makes this point succinctly:

> Indeed, the core underlying thread of this entire analysis has been that professions are first and foremost a system of work, and to ask what it is that makes a profession more or less professional is to inquire into the system of practice by which that work gets done. Recruitment, policy, leadership, budgets, and school

organization are all important, to be sure, but to focus on these issues while ignoring the primary mechanisms by which professions manage and control their work is to lose sight of what is most central to any professional enterprise—a system of practice. (p. 184)

It's all about "how the work gets done." The system of practice that is central to the work of teachers is their engaging as members of a team of professionals working collaboratively to solve the challenges of instruction they face in their daily work and use those collaborative meetings as an opportunity to learn and refine their practice. Teachers must take charge of that system of practice, the professional learning community, to make a real difference in how they operate as teachers so that student learning improves. As they take more control over their professional lives, the need for traditional employee unions and directives from politicians and supervisors begins to diminish.

Beyond the Catchphrase . . .

To live in the world without becoming aware of the meaning of the world is
like wandering about in a great library without touching the books.

Dan Brown, *The Lost Symbol* (2009)

ONE OF THIS BOOK'S AUTHORS recently moved from a large
metropolitan city—population: 1,500,000—to a small rural village of
11,000—a beautiful, hilly, horse-oriented region. The streets are full
of pickup trucks, horse trailers, and other vehicles proclaiming their owners'
association with the earth/soil of the region. Our author made attempts to
raise a small crop of tomatoes and herbs in a sunny, raised-earth area of the
new home. Meeting with an abysmal lack of success, she engaged the local
rural extension agent in obtaining samples of the soil to send to the nearby
university for analysis and advice.

The results of these analyses were to be distributed at a meeting of local farmers, where the university's representative would lecture on fertilizers.
Our author was invited to this event and went down the highway 20 miles to
the local community's high school Ag Center. Here, the participants, in the
main, included men in their 50s wearing their jeans, "gimme" caps or straw
hats, and very sturdy work shoes/boots. One guy even had that picturesque,
horizontally long mustache, waxed and twirled at the ends.

This group had, for the most part, succeeded recently in harvesting a
spectacular hay crop, due to a warm summer and abundant rains at the appropriate time. But they were concerned about how to effectively manage
their next crops. They had, thus, asked for this meeting and its topic so they
could learn about fertilizers.

Now, what does this bunch of farmers have to do with professional learning community? Actually, quite a lot: They have a regular time and location
for meeting, they come together (in a group, in community) with frequency
in order to access learning for themselves about a topic they determine, and
that is destined to improve their outcomes—in this case, a continuously successful hay crop. Are they professionals? You bet! We would not be enjoying

last night's terrific steak dinner without their involvement. Some of these guys were even getting CEUs (continuing education units) for their attendance and involvement, as they are certified in pesticide licensing.

Do they constitute a PLC? Indeed—yes.

Would they label themselves as such? Indeed—no. They've never heard the term.

Interestingly, there are large numbers of schools and districts across this nation, labeling themselves as professional learning communities (PLC). Do they constitute a PLC? Let's see.

WHAT WE READ, SEE, AND HEAR

Like any new idea, strategy, or approach that has become the "innovation du jour," PLCs have been defined and operationalized in multiple ways by well-meaning practitioners, some of whom are consistently looking for the next new idea or innovation. There appears to be wide divergence between what is reported in research studies of professional learning communities, what many practitioners share and describe as their practice of PLC, and what some PLC consultants, committed to the success of all students, write for their constituents.

Research on PLC

In Chapter 2, from a brief description of the research base on professional learning community, five descriptors, attributes, or components were reported. These five items, with the fourth item (supportive conditions) now divided for better specificity and understanding, serve to explicate the identity of effective PLCs. Briefly, these are:

Supportive and shared leadership that expresses the school campus and district administrators' sharing of power and authority through sharing decision-making with the staff;

Shared beliefs, values, and vision that are grounded in the community's unrelenting commitment to student learning;

Intentional collective learning by the community that is applied in classrooms to benefit student learning;

Physical or structural conditions, and provision of resources, that support the community in meeting to do their learning work;

Collegial or relational conditions that encourage and build the
    atmosphere for collective learning; and
Shared practice in which teachers invite and are invited to visit, observe,
    take notes, and consult with one another about their classroom
    practice, in the spirit of individual and community improvement, so
    students learn more successfully.

It doesn't take magic to understand that these research-based conditions
and actions do not develop or occur overnight, or over a semester, but require
long-term time and effort in development. Meanwhile, numerous variations
of the PLC evolve as the PLC has been introduced and efforts are made to
implement the structure/strategy.

Reports from the Field

Because of our interest, readings, writings, keynote addresses, and large-
group learning sessions (workshops), we have had the opportunity to gain information about the status of PLC in many schools and school districts. Many
of these schools have shared with us, in addition to our observations, a great
deal of information about what teachers and school administrators are doing
when they are "doing it." These informal reports may be categorized in three
types of descriptions.

"We meet." The most basic requirement of a community of professional
learners is the time and place to meet. With great frequency, informers share
with us that their school, grade level, or academic department meets regularly. In attempts to promote further disclosure, queries about what the participants are doing when they are meeting is met with blank faces, or lack of
any verbal response.

Certainly, having an identified schedule of time and a location to meet is
a basic element of the PLC. It is not hard to imagine, because school faculties
have not very often had the time allowed and the possibility to meet, that this
first requirement *is* the innovation—that is, the opportunity to come together.
It is not clear if campus administrators assume that staff know what/how to
use the time given to them, or if the administrator him/herself is not well
informed about what the community might, or should, be doing when they
meet. In cases where we have been informed that the community has a time
and place to meet, there seems to be little understanding about or intention
of what to do further. Where insufficient time, attention, and resources have

been provided, new popular reform ideas are often relegated to the graveyard of failure, as noted by Sarason (1993).

We believe that the "We meet" PLCs have a long row to hoe in order to grow into a community of professional learners.

"We work collaboratively." Collaboration, currently, has become a benchmark of the espoused PLC. Again, it would appear that the term *community* has taken up prominent residence in the minds of many schools and their consulting supporters/supporting consultants. Certainly, working collaboratively is necessary for the community's learning, but it is the means, not the end.

Across the nation there appears to be abundant discourse about PLCs working collaboratively: creating common assessments, providing intervention where data study indicates such a need. Seldom is there any note of the requisite teachers' learning about how to create common assessments, or of learning the intervention and how to use it. One wonders whether it is assumed that they already have this knowledge and skill—if so, one would wonder why these practices had not been put into operation earlier. If they are not in the knowledge base and skill sets of teachers, how do teachers develop the deep content knowledge and practice the envisioned skills, to employ in support of student learning? Working collaboratively sounds like a desired activity, but where and how is the learning required of faculty to be able to use new practices? It's a thorny question.

It is possible that the identified learning that the community has determined they need can be accessed from a member of the community. If this is not the case, then the community looks outside its membership, across the school, in an effort to find help. If help is not available within the school, then the community looks to another school, or to a district office. If these explorations return negative results, then looking to the state or regional area for consultation may be required.

When we visited a north-central state several years ago, we learned that the state Standards Task Force had just identified a new skill for students: As students completed the computation and response to an open-ended mathematics question, they were to verbalize their thinking as they solved the problem, then they were to write a paragraph to report in text how and why they had approached the problem as they did. Teachers and principals judged that this skill was quite good for students. However, they soon discovered one problem: They could find no teacher or administrator who could support and enable the teachers to develop this skill in students. Widening their search externally, the educators finally identified a national consultant several states removed, who could and would come to help them learn how to teach their students, so that students could master this standard.

Although it is fortunate to find a "teacher of teachers" internally or nearby, it may not always be possible. Most certainly, it is not a good idea to use available help that is inadequate or may confirm poor practice.

While the "We work collaboratively" PLC is a step in the right direction, there seems to be an absence of the adult learning that will support educators in adopting new practice and becoming proficient with its use, resulting in more effective educators.

"We engage in continuous cycles of school improvement." The professional learning community concept and practice is, essentially, a strong structure and strategy for improving classroom and school effectiveness, and subsequently, student performance. We believe that it is the most powerful strategy that we have for improving our schools—if done well.

For years, educators have been promoting the use of a protocol, or steps, for engaging in continuous school improvement. These steps typically include:

From the study of an array of student performance data, identify area(s) of student need;

Select the most critical need, and create student learning goals based on the learning expectations in state standards;

Explore options and specify the most promising instructional approach to address the need;

Plan and deliver instruction to students;

Assess to determine degree of student progress, and refine;

Re-teach, review, refine, re-teach and/or repeat the cycle as student goals are met.

Protocols such as this are widely touted as a means to direct the PLC work and study—*if a protocol is available.* Nowhere in this protocol, nor in many others that we have been privileged to review, has community members' professional learning, related to the instructional strategy adopted, been *explicitly* included as an action step. This has been the case for decades in the school improvement realm, and now appears to be the case with PLC dogma.

While professional development, or professional learning, has been given widespread lip service as a necessity for improving educators' practice, and while this factor is given attention in the school change literature, still no real emphasis in the change literature has been placed on the importance of this factor. There can be no improvement in our schools without changing what is not working for students' successful learning and replacing it with programs or practices that have the potential for increased student performance. Such changes cannot occur without educators learning what the new "way" is, and how to use it. This means that professional learning is clearly a mandate for change and improvement, although this has not been so readily apparent to many school reformers.

If school improvement is

- dependent on identifying what is not working and eliminating that;
- exchanging for a potentially promising strategy; and
- learning how to use the adopted strategy,

how can improvement succeed, if the learning piece of the equation is absent?

One wonders about the effectiveness of the "We engage in continuous cycles of school improvement" models currently in vogue. Let us look to a new articulation–the cycle of continuous improvement with a focus on adult learning.

SCHOOL IMPROVEMENT AND THE WORK OF THE COMMUNITY

Thirty years ago, Lucianne Carmichael opined that "the teacher is the first learner" (quoted in Hord, 2004, p. 14), meaning that students could not learn more than their teachers' repertoires provided, and that teachers must first learn new content and strategies to increase their effectiveness so that students' learning improved (Does this remind us of educational professionals?). Carmichael's school was one of the early models of the PLC, and an exemplar. From the review of research studies and conversations with leaders of what appear to be effective PLCs, we have concluded that the "work of the community" (Hord & Hirsh, 2008, pp. 36–38) being used in these communities looks like Figure 4.1, a streamlined shirt-pocket reminder card of the steps of "The 10-Step Work of the Community of Professional Learners."

The community initiates its work through the examination of a wide array of student performance data to assess the productivity of their teaching, and how those data indicate student needs, or areas where students are not learning well. As a community, they then use the steps in Figure 4.1 to guide their community work.

Figure 4.1. The 10–Step Work of the Community of Professional Learners

1. Reflect on our work for students and determine whether it is producing desired results.

2. Refer to our data to ascertain where students are learning well and where they are not.

3. Identify student learning areas in need of attention.

4. Specify priority areas and determine those that require immediate attention.

5. Study solutions that address our students' needs and decide new practice(s) to adopt.

6. Commit to learning the new practices in order to employ them effectively.

7. Determine what we will need to learn and how we will design our learning.

8. Plan collegially for implementing our new learning in our classrooms.

9. Assess implementation, adjust if necessary; analyze the effects of new practices on our students' learning.

10. Revise and adjust where necessary; celebrate students' success, and continue the cycle.

Do these steps stimulate a picture of mature, committed, responsible educators dedicating the time and effort to serve all clients well? We think so! Taking a shortcut, we can rather easily understand professional learning community, simply by defining the three words that make up the term:

Professionals = those licensed or certified to have mastered a body of knowledge and a set of skills; in the educational setting, these individuals are thought of as those who are responsible and accountable for delivering a high-quality instructional program for students.

Community = individuals who come together to share and support or promote an agreed-upon or common goal.

Learning = mastering new content, skills, behaviors, and/or approaches with their related application.

An interesting thought occurs: Professional learning communities have widely demonstrated a deep concern and study of student data. In addition, these teams or communities have expressed a deep and consistent focus on student learning. One might wonder whether the "learning" in the professional learning community label is thought of, by some PLC members, as student learning rather than adult learning. To ensure student learning, the PLC must look first to its own professional learning.

THE CONTINUUM OF PROFESSIONAL PRACTICE

There appears to be a progression in how teachers work together. It's a real challenge for teachers who are comfortable working in isolation to instantly become members of a professional learning community. When we've worked with teachers who have little experience sharing with their peers, we've found that meeting together to plan can be a first step on the road to developing a community of learners. We never abandon the idea of having teachers see all opportunities to meet as opportunities to learn. We found that Figure 4.2, the "Continuum of Professional Practice" (pp. 46–47), is a useful tool to help teachers and principals understand the differences between meeting just to share and meeting in a professional learning community.

Five vertical factors (actions, context, teacher learning, relation to student learning, and application of learning) are used to describe what teachers would be doing in each of the structural arrangements provided on the horizontal continuum. For example, the teacher learning factor indicates what or how teachers would be learning as they advance across the structures from left to right. Information is also provided about the relation to student learning that is either incidental or purposeful. One of the factors that makes the greatest difference in whether a practice is truly professional is how learning is applied. In professional learning communities, teachers hold one another accountable for applying what they have learned as a team, which is a far cry from teachers meeting together with no accountability for applying what they may have learned.

However, this continuum does not sufficiently explain what a PLC looks like in action. But an innovation configuration map can provide a useful and clarifying guide.

MAPPING PROFESSIONAL LEARNING COMMUNITIES

The innovation configuration map was created by researchers at the Research and Development Center for Teacher Education at the University of Texas, Austin. Investigating the conditions and needs of education staff, PK–16, to adopt and implement change in order to improve their practice for student benefit, researchers found wide disparity in the understanding among public school teachers/university faculty and administrators, across and within schools, about just *what* the new practice was. More often than not, when staff members were interviewed, they expressed interest in using "the new way" but didn't know for sure what that really meant.

Recognizing this problem, the research team initiated work to correct this dilemma faced by change leaders in their organizations. The result was a rubric-type instrument that identified the major pieces, parts, or components of any program, process, or practice—in other words, a map of the innovation (Hall & Hord, 2011, Chapter 3).

This first step in constructing an IC map is an analysis step typically quite challenging to those not experienced in such skills (Hord, Stiegelbauer, Hall, & George, 2006). Once the components (or, as some prefer to label them, the "desired outcome") have been established, each component is initially described by its most desirable behaviors (as the map is an instrument that describes the innovation in operation, in action).

This description appears as Variation 1 (or Level 1). Decreasing value descriptions are offered across a continuum that will depict the likely images from more to less successful levels of the innovation in operation in classrooms (or wherever the appropriate setting may be). Variation 1 is the "best practice," or "exemplary practice" of the component. It serves as the goal of implementation and sets the final expectations for implementation of the innovation. At the same time, Variations 2, 3, 4, and so on allow for less "elegant" behaviors as the implementers are learning about the innovation and how to use it. We understand the IC map as "a growth-inducing tool" because it enables both the implementer and the change facilitator to have (truly) a map to guide them in their activities in pursuit of implementation.

Figure 4.3 (pp. 48–53) presents an IC map that we have designed that explicitly identifies and specifies what the members of the community will be doing while in a PLC. The principal and any other designated staff will be part of the community; thus, they will be guided by the map. We have taken the six components from the synthesis of research on professional learning communities (reported in Chapter 2) as the source for this map. This map constitutes our operational definition of PLC through the IC map of what teachers and administrators do when participating in a PLC.

As suggested above, the source for this map is the research-based components of a professional learning community. And, as noted, "the PLC member" includes the teachers and administrators of the school. The component is stated above the continuum in action terms. *The PLC Member* is the subject. When each of the verb-initiated phrases is read with "The PLC Member" in front of it, a complete sentence is expressed. The number 1 description under the component heading is the highest-quality, or the "best practices," description. Increasingly less desirable or lower-quality descriptions follow across the continuum.

In this way, the number 1 descriptions for each component articulate precisely what effective PLC members are doing in their community work.

text continues on p. 54

Figure 4.2. Continuum of Professional Practice

Structure	Teachers operate in isolation	Teachers meet to plan together	Teachers share tips, tricks, and techniques
Actions	Individual planning that may or may not address student needs	Teachers compare notes about what they'll be teaching	Teachers meet during planning time and share ideas they've read or heard about
Context	Leave me alone to teach	Here's what I'm teaching next week	Here's a good idea that worked for me—you should try it
Teacher Learning	Some new learning possible but very individualistic	Planning meetings result in little new learning, if any	Sharing conversations are often superficial with little thought about whether the ideas have any research base or support
Relation to Student Learning	Incidental	Incidental	Incidental
Application of Learning	Any new learning that has occurred may or may not be applied	Lessons are taught but there's no expectation that results of lessons (student learning) will be shared	Teachers sharing ideas hold no expectations that their ideas must be implemented by others

Figure 4.2. Continuum of Professional Practice *(continued)*

Structure	Teachers engage in a book study	Teachers engage in study groups	Professional Learning Community	
Actions	Often, the book is chosen by a formal or informal leader	Based on student test data teachers select a topic to pursue and learn about	Focus of the learning emanates from a review of ongoing evidence of student learning	Teachers Operating as True Professionals
Context	Let's read this book together and see what we get from it	Let's examine the impact that our teaching has had on student learning	Let's examine the impact that our teaching has had on student learning	
Teacher Learning	The new learning is associated with the book topic only and may or may not be generalized to inform teaching practice	The new learning is associated with the study group topic and may or may not be generalized to inform teaching practice	Learning is rich and focused on addressing content and applying research-based strategies stemming from a review of student work and reflection about the impact that instruction has had on student learning	
Relation to Student Learning	Incidental	Purposeful	Purposeful	
Application of Learning	Any new learning that has occurred may or may not be applied	Accountability for application comes from an instructional council rather than the group itself	Members of a PLC hold one another accountable for applying what they've learned together, discussing the results and agreeing on how to adjust instruction based on those results	

Figure 4.3. Innovation Configuration Map for the Professional Learning Community

The PLC Member:

Component A: Shares the responsibility for leading the work of a professional learning community.				
1	2	3	4	5
Seeks or accepts the role and responsibility for leading the work of a PLC; promotes the identification and assignment of potential leadership roles for PLC colleagues; develops insights and suggestions for creating leadership roles for others; shares possibilities for leadership equitably with other members of the PLC; participates in decision-making based on sound judgment.	Accepts, although initially tentative, a role and responsibility for guiding and supporting the PLC's work; shares insights and suggestions for creating leadership roles, and promotes the assignment of potential roles for PLC colleagues; shares possibilities for leadership equitably with other PLC members.	Assumes PLC leadership roles reluctantly; promotes assigning such roles to other PLC colleagues; begins to feel comfortable playing a role in leading the PLC.	Avoids taking leadership roles; lobbies consistently for the same colleagues to take roles in leading the PLC.	Fails to consider self as a leader; gives little to no attention to this role and its value in the PLC.

Component B: Expresses and shares a school vision focused on teacher and student learning.

1	2	3	4	5
Articulates own personal beliefs and values; discusses these with impunity and to gain consensus; uses the consensus to collegially formulate a vision for the school that relentlessly focuses on adult and student learning; provides energy and enthusiasm for sharing and promoting the vision to colleagues, and to school and neighborhood communities.	Shares his/her vision of the school's purpose; energetically promotes his/her vision, but collaborates to gain consensus for the school's vision that highlights educator and students' continuous learning; plans with colleagues to promote the vision with parents.	Supports the school's vision that focuses on student learning; maintains communication with parents that reports events and activities that enable the school to realize its vision.	Forgets that the school has a vision; neglects to apply it personally and fails to share the vision with the school's constituency.	

Figure 4.3. Innovation Configuration Map for the Professional Learning Community *(continued)*

Component C: Engages in continuous intentional and collective learning.				
1	2	3	4	5
Explores a wide variety of student data sources to identify areas of students' needs for improvement; establishes, with colleagues, a focus for change in teaching/learning practices that address students' needs; determines collaboratively what teachers will need to learn; decides collectively how teachers will do this learning; participates in the learning; plans with the PLC members how new practice will be implemented in classrooms and how student learning will be assessed; uses evidence of student learning to review, assess, and revise implementation activities and adjusts instruction based on that review.	Uses multiple data sources to identify areas of students' low performance; determines a priority focus for change in instructional practice, targeting students' needs; delineates what teachers will need to learn related to the new practice, and how they will do the learning; participates in the learning and planning to transfer new practice to classrooms.	Uses a variety of multiple data sources to identify areas of students' low performance; specifies change(s) that will increase student performance; identifies the learning that teachers will need to accomplish; participates in the learning.	Employs state achievement tests as the basis for determining action to take to address students' poor performance; works with PLC colleagues to plan and take action.	Uses the PLC meeting time for planning with colleagues for materials and other resources for teaching the established units of study; discusses which resources to order, but no further conversation is devoted to instruction.

Component D: Provides, receives, and uses feedback on classroom teaching/learning practices.				
1	2	3	4	5
Invites colleagues to observe specified teaching activity and to provide feedback that will be used to change and enhance practice; visits colleagues on invitation to observe and offer feedback; responds to hosting colleagues and visiting colleagues on the schedule and direction of the principal; shares expertise and instructional ideas with colleagues during PLC meetings, their lunch hour, planning time, and after school; reflects on his/her practices and related feedback, and adjusts.	Invites and schedules PLC colleagues to observe and provide feedback on a specific teaching activity; visits colleagues on invitation to observe and offer feedback for improvement; shares successful teaching activities informally during PLC meetings, at the lunch hour, during planning time, and after school.	Serves as host and as visiting teacher, inviting colleagues to observe specific activities in order to share feedback; provides feedback when requested to others; shares expertise with other members.	Shares lessons and classroom activities that students enjoyed.	

Figure 4.3. Innovation Configuration Map for the Professional Learning Community *(continued)*

Component E: Uses structures and schedules to advance the PLC's work.				
1	2	3	4	5
Solicits the scheduling of a regular and frequent time for the PLC to meet; seeks a comfortable and available space for the PLC's regular meetings; articulates, with colleagues, norms that share expectations and guide the community's behaviors; appears on time and prepared for the PLC's meetings; uses the time and meeting space for engaging in the learning work of the PLC; encourages colleagues in their participation.	Persuades administrators to find/create time for regular PLC meetings; surveys the staff to identify a location for the regular meetings of the PLC; arrives on time and prepared for engaging in the meeting's shared agenda.	Implores administrators to identify the time for regular PLC meetings; pleads for a comfortable and regular location to be identified for the PLC meetings.	Takes no action in behalf of the scheduling and other structures to make it possible to meet.	

Component F: Participates in the development and application of relationship factors in support of the PLC's work.

1	2	3	4	5
Approaches the initial PLC meetings eagerly with an open (and receiving) mind and heart; articulates and endorses team/PLC learning in order to become more effective; promotes positive PLC relationships through both pleasant and productive interactions; exhibits trustworthiness through delivering on promises; demonstrates regard for colleagues and respect for their ideas and suggestions.	Encourages colleagues enthusiastically regarding the initial meetings and endorses their potential for increased teacher effectiveness, student learning, and staff morale; increases positive PLC relationships through consistent pleasant and productive conversations and activity; delivers on promises and demonstrates trustworthiness; expresses regard for colleagues.	Promotes colleagues' attendance and participation at meetings through persistent, but pleasant, reminders of the potential benefits and pleasurable interactions; shares pleasant conversations focused on adult and student learning to promote harmony; serves as a buffer when conversations veer unpleasantly; congratulates colleagues on both large and small "conquests."	Demonstrates pleasant interactions and exemplifies reliability, dependability, and transparency.	

CONCLUDING THOUGHTS

Change requires learning; learning results in change. When the adults are engaged in the learning, students can be direct beneficiaries . . . and student outcomes can be created. Adult learning linked to student learning results in benefits to both staff and students. Such benefits include:

Increased staff learning that accesses deep content knowledge and a repertoire of instructional strategies that result in more effective classroom instruction;

A shift in the thinking of teachers and administrators as they become continuous reflective practitioners, always exploring alternatives for increased teaching and learning performance, and enhancing their professional posture;

Greater respect, efficacy, and professional identity of the PLC members for themselves, their colleagues, and the profession; and

Enhanced, enriched, improved student performance.

CHAPTER FIVE

What Educators *Do* in a Professional Learning Community

If a child can't learn the way we teach, maybe we should teach the way they learn.

Ignacio Estrada

WE HAVE HAD THE GREAT FORTUNE to work with schools that are implementing PLCs and our experience in those schools has influenced our thinking about how engaging in authentic PLCs encourages professionalism. We have seen firsthand how shared leadership has opened the door for teachers to take charge of their own learning and take mutual responsibility for student learning. We've been witness to the culture of a school shifting from teachers working in isolation to teachers being open and honest about what they need to learn and supporting one another's learning. We've also seen that it takes more than the NSDC Learning Community Standard stating, "Teacher members of learning teams, which consist of four to eight members, assist one another in examining the standards students are required to master, planning more effective lessons, critiquing student work, and solving the common problems of teaching" (National Staff Development Council, 2001). The Innovation Configuration Maps for the NSDC Standards for Staff Development (Roy & Hord, 2003) and the new Innovation Configuration Map we've created for PLCs (see Figure 4.2) take that brief statement and provide a picture of a professional learning community in practice.

To fill in that picture of what teachers and others do in a professional learning community with more detail, we describe what happened in three schools in which we have worked.

HIGH PLAINS ELEMENTARY: THE *WORK* OF A PLC

In this small school district of nine schools—one high school, one middle school, six elementary schools, and an alternative secondary school—school teams consisting of the principal, the assistant principal, and one or two teacher leaders (depending on the size of the school) attended 12 large-group learning sessions (workshops) scheduled every other month over the course of 2 years. The daylong workshops focused on renewing or confirming the knowledge and skills of school leaders for guiding their PLCs. These work-shops were followed by application assignments in the schools, in which edu-cators applied what they had learned in the workshops that preceded. The assignments included activities specifically related to the goal of the learning session, such as:

> *Goal:* Identify teachers' concerns and provide actions to support their work with the new reading program.
>
> *Directions:* Identify six teachers randomly in the school and 1) use the interview protocol that we studied in our learning session to elicit each teacher's most intense concern about the reading program that was the focus of implementation; 2) generate a supportive intervention for each teacher and deliver it to him/her; 3) make a chart of the six teachers, showing a column for their name and grade level, a column for their concern, and on the same horizontal line, state the intervention provided; make a fourth column for effect that we will explore next month.
>
> *Goal:* Create an "elevator speech" that will explain crisply to parents or others what a professional learning community is and its purpose.
>
> *Directions:* With a partner, 1) make a brief outline, with notes, that defines a professional learning community; 2) check your definition with the materials from our learning session; 3) each person will practice delivering the speech to the other; 4) the other person will share feedback with the presenting partner; 5) switch roles and repeat the process; 6) conduct the process again and time the presentations (they should be no longer than 4 minutes).

While schools worked on the assignment during the month subsequent to the workshop, the consultant and a central office staff person visited the campuses to interact with the school teams: asking questions, answering questions, clarifying uncertainties regarding the material under study, clarifying the assignments, and reviewing the assigned work at the school site. The next monthly workshop would process this experience to develop new knowledge, understandings, insights, and skills with the school teams, before directing attention to new material and learning. The goal was to support and assist the schools in developing professional learning communities.

During one of the consultants' monthly site visit trips at the beginning of the second year, the 1st-grade learning team in one of the schools invited her to their community's meeting to observe what they were doing. Sitting with the team in a circle of 1st-grade chairs where one's elbows touch one's knees, the consultant asked the group, "What is the focus of your learning?"

Without hesitation, several responded in unison, "A new way to teach creative writing."

"Why are you learning about that?"

"Because our student state achievement data showed that students in the school were consistently falling below proficiency over time as they moved from kindergarten to 4th grade. Further, our students' writing products were not what we hoped they would be."

"Ah, so what and how are you doing your learning?"

Such an interesting group of 1st-grade teachers, each of them responding to questions and adding to their colleagues' comments! The consultant requested that they tell her their story of how they initiated the work of their community and were engaged in new learning about how to teach creative writing to 1st-graders.

Early Steps

Our story began in July of the previous summer when the principal received the school's annual achievement scores. Putting the data into a readily accessible format and making multiple copies, the principal invited the teachers to bring their swimsuits to the neighborhood club and come for a day of relaxing, having lunch, and studying their data. One member of the staff was enrolled in summer school and couldn't manipulate his schedule; another was backpacking in the California Rockies and was absent. But the remainder of the faculty was there.

They meticulously created and used a protocol to review and study the data, sharing directions and the leadership of the group. They first observed where students had performed well, vowing to celebrate with a small event on the first day of the fall semester. Then they turned their attention to the areas where students had not achieved well, and identified mathematics as problematic. Exploring more deeply, the primary grade teachers, in addition to the 4th-grade teachers, discovered that their students' writing scores "were in the pits." A problem: What to do? What to address?

The principal insisted that it would not be a good strategy to undertake multiple improvement efforts simultaneously. Furthermore, she reminded them, they were well into the third year of a focus on reading and it appeared that gains were just ahead, that they had a good handle on their new reading curriculum, and could continue that with the help of the instructional guide to support them in evaluating their students' progress in reading. She asked the staff to consider digging deeper into their students' difficulties with subtraction in math and to explore the students' challenges with story writing in order to generate a list of factors that might be contributing to these two areas of disappointment. She requested they bring a report to a meeting during the staff's August pre-semester readiness days.

As a result of their investigation, several teachers discovered and reported at the school-wide staff meeting that the materials for their students' math instruction were not appropriate for the students' level of understanding and the differentiated instructional program the teachers were implementing. They were appalled that they had not noted this earlier, and admitted that they had been quite frustrated with the resources at hand. The group determined that they would reallocate the materials so that all teachers would have the necessary resources that were required for the differentiated mathematics instruction they were implementing. Furthermore, they planned several meetings with the math consultant to review the strategies for teaching subtraction in a constructivist approach. Feeling more confident after identifying the source of their concerns about mathematics and having made these adjustments for their resources and plans for additional professional mathematics learning, the teachers then met in their grade-level teams to scrutinize the writing problem in depth, to better understand what the root of the problem might be.

Moving Along

The 1st-grade team was one of the teams that had been having the hard conversations about their knowledge and skills regarding the teaching of math. Unlike some of the other grade-level teams, they had accessed the help of the math instructional guide, who had worked with them for several weeks to assist them in instructional strategies to use with their students. This professional learning for the teachers resulted in their increased confidence for teaching math.

Because they had developed a good deal of trust in one another, they acknowledged that they weren't really confident about teaching writing, and since the district had no curriculum guides for writing, they had been flying rather blindly with their teaching of creative writing to their students. Their consternation and open conversation resulted in their decision to invite both the principal and the district office elementary curriculum director to their next meeting in order to identify options for addressing their situation. They realized that collectively they didn't know how to help themselves or one another.

When the curriculum director and principal met with the team, the group's agenda was to specify which 1st-grade writing standards were most in need of attention, and to set goals to focus their actions for achieving the standards. The curriculum director proved to be exceptionally helpful in assisting the team to identify standards. The principal, who several years in the past had taught others the skills of the New Jersey Writing Project, made a significant contribution in her suggestions for writing programs and processes that could be considered. After weeks of study and several meetings with their two advisors, the team decided to take on the Abc/Xyz Writing program whose goals matched those that they wished for their students.

The team committed to a yearlong agenda for their own learning: what the new program was and how to teach it. The professional development was so designed that short portions of the program could be studied, plans could be made by the team for transferring their learning to classroom instruction, and then the plans tried in their classrooms. The team debriefed these lessons, explored their students' work in a team meeting, revised the lessons, and tried them again. They also created a schedule, at the principal's suggestion, whereby they could visit one another's classrooms to observe the host teacher using the writing program with students. The visiting teacher scripted notes from his/her observations; later in the day, they met to share, discuss, and assess strategies—another avenue for their intentional learning.

Their intense study, focused on a specific topic in a social setting, provided significant learning for them, where they could explain, describe, inquire, discuss, and even debate. Simultaneously, sharing and suggesting applications of their learning in their classrooms was very powerful for them. In a word, they learned a great deal that increased their effectiveness as teachers committed to students' learning.

They continued to plan for implementing their new knowledge and skills in their classrooms, monitoring how faithfully they were transferring their community learning to the classroom, and, taking care through investigating students' work, monitoring how well the new practices were influencing students' learning. As a result of their continuous sharing and learning with and from one another and their two consultants, they revisited their planning and implementation strategies, revising and adjusting as they deemed necessary.

The visitor asked one more question of the 1st-grade learning team: "How are you aligning your new learning and classroom work with the other grade-level communities in your school?"

The teachers looked somewhat sheepishly at one another, but responded that they had been so consumed with their own students and their own learning in order to teach more effectively that they had not thought about what others were doing.

"Of course," they said, "there must be continuous alignment of the writing curriculum, knowledge, and skills, so that is where we will focus our attention next—and invite our elementary curriculum director to help us address this issue."

DESERT RIVER MIDDLE SCHOOL

The district in which this middle school is located is similar in size to the district of High Plains. Desert River Middle is one of two middle schools in a K–8 district with six elementary schools on the roster. This district is situated in the southwest at the border of Mexico, and is thereby challenged by the needs of English Language Learners, as a very high percentage of the students' native language is Spanish. As you might imagine, this language challenge influences much of the students' learning, including reading and writing. The faculty laments continuously about it, but is not seeking solutions.

Charting a New Course

Principal Gonzales, Assistant Principal Johnston, and Reading Specialist Sweeney huddled together early one August morning to come to grips with this situation. They knew that the staff recognized the poor performance of their students in reading especially, but as yet had not been catalyzed to action. How to develop a sense of urgency with the staff and an instructional approach that seemed to promise reasonable success, they thought, was critical.

After several cups of coffee and unremarkable discussion, Reading Specialist Sweeney suddenly remembered and shared that she had attended a reading conference during the summer where one school reported how the staff had developed a reading-across-all-content-areas program, and that they were getting results! This stimulated interest and encouraged the small group to gain additional information. Specialist Sweeney promised to look into this program and to report back in a week at their regularly scheduled meeting.

As a result of interacting with one of the conference participants, Specialist Sweeney came to the next meeting brimming with energy and enthusiasm; she had an idea for their situation. She reminded her teammates of the abysmal reading scores of their students at all grades and subjects, to which they nodded in agreement. To address the problem broadside, she suggested that they engage all faculty members, including the physical education staff, in conducting a daily reading lesson at the start of the day.

Including all staff would signal the importance of the activity, not only to teachers but also to students. A weekly "unit" of five lessons, one for each day of the school week, would be created on a rotating basis by each subject-matter department team, in addition to the administrative team. These lessons would address the following:

Day 1 would focus on vocabulary definition and enhancement;

Day 2 would address reading comprehension and how the author developed the story or article parts;

Day 3 would be used to teach the students word attack skills, and how to infer comprehension when explicit detail was not provided;

Day 4 would be used to address author's voice, or how s/he created tone or feeling, as the context for the written piece;

Day 5 was committed to teachers evaluating student outcomes for the week and gaining evidence of students' achievement, which would be useful for planning.

Each team would be responsible for encouraging the staff in their department to use the materials that they had designed and prepared. But first, Specialist Sweeney stated, the entire staff must be provided with professional learning in order to gain basic knowledge and skills for teaching reading.

The administrative team volunteered to create the first set of materials and to conduct a "campaign" to engage the interest and participation of all teachers. They announced a 3-hour event that included a barbecue lunch to occur in 2 weeks on a district-scheduled professional development day. Specialist Sweeney geared up to construct materials to teach the faculty how to teach reading and to provide notebooks for creating the weekly lessons. Assistant Principal Johnston invited students to design T-shirts for the staff, proclaiming "Each Teacher a Teacher of Reading." The "buzz" about this new program was building as everyone engaged in rumor, gossip, and hearsay about the new activity.

Addressing everyone's comfort level, Specialist Sweeney, at the 3-hour event, provided the staff with initial professional learning focused on vocabulary development using "word walls" for adolescent readers and a review of how to use the dictionary and its tools that support the reader in comprehending particular words that they will encounter in the written text. These easy-to-understand lessons launched the program. Specialist Sweeney shared a schedule of short, twice-a-week professional learning sessions with the staff that ensured they would be able to start the program with sufficient skills. They were promised that Sweeney would be available to coach the staff in order to continually improve their teaching skills. Principal Gonzales, meanwhile, was reporting their plan to the superintendent and to the parents at their regular monthly meeting to solicit understanding and support. He constructed the schedule for the daily 45-minute reading lesson, ensured that all teachers of each department had common meeting times available . . . and checked on the progress of the T-shirt production.

Launching the Program

The administrative team polished the lesson plans for the first set of reading lessons. Each of the academic department teams, when developing the plans for the staff, had the responsibility of selecting the topic and a short text for the first day's lesson in vocabulary. The administrative team selected a short history of the school, and created additional materials for teaching reading skills on the topic for the remaining 4 days of the week. This set of lessons was the focus of professional learning as a rehearsal the week before the "launch" of the program.

Initially, the staff was doubtful about their ability to teach reading. But knowing that all the teachers were involved, as well as the administrators, and with all members of the staff appreciating the clever graphics and rainbow colors of their T-shirts, they gamely participated.

As the program settled in, department team members began sharing their learning with teammates, and working together creatively to plan their week's lessons—always knowing that Specialist Sweeney and the language arts department staff were available for assistance and support.

After several months, two state department of education personnel were visiting in the building and asked the principal about the program. Principal Gonzales called two students randomly from the hallway and asked them to describe their new program. They did so with enthusiasm and accuracy. It was clear that students and teachers were involved and sharing with one another their experiences with this program that was being experienced by everyone in the school.

Without labeling it as such, and without knowing it, the department teams were becoming small learning communities, with the whole school serving as a full-staff community of professional learners.

LOW COUNTRY MIDDLE SCHOOL

Over the course of 2 years, SEDL (formerly Southwest Educational Development Laboratory) worked with two school districts in the South to deepen the learning that occurred during their common planning time. One middle school in particular embraced the partnership wholeheartedly. SEDL introduced a process called the Professional Teaching and Learning Cycle (PTLC) that was developed by SEDL in partnership with the Charles A. Dana Center at the University of Texas, Austin.

The Professional Teaching and Learning Cycle (PTLC) serves as a protocol that guides the work of teachers as they engage in the process of continuous professional learning described in Chapter 4. The PTLC (defined in Table 5.1 and Figure 5.1, pp. 64–65) expects that teachers will work in collaborative teams to develop a common understanding of what they need to teach, how to teach those concepts, how to determine whether their teaching was effective, and how to adjust instruction based on what they've learned. The process does more than promote an interesting dialogue about teaching and learning. As teachers are developing a "common understanding," they are exploring new ways of looking at student learning expectations and researching best practices for teaching those learning expectations. They hold one another accountable for results, and they bring back to their team evidence of student learning from the lessons they taught. When they examine that evidence, they work together to address student misconceptions or lack of understanding of the concepts taught. If they don't have all the answers, they look outside their group to find additional resources and information about how to proceed. In short, they are learning what they need to do to become more effective teachers.

Before SEDL introduced the PTLC to the district, the schools had already set aside planning time for teachers. They had received training in the use of data and had begun to chart student progress using benchmark data rather than a single, end-of-the-year measure of academic achievement. Planning time most often consisted of teachers sharing which section of the textbook they would be teaching next and occasionally suggesting a clever technique to their colleagues. Data were available but were discussed only once or twice during the year and were rarely used to inform instruction. The planning meetings rarely consisted of a deep analysis of teaching practice that would

text continues on p. 66

Table 5.1. The Professional Teaching and Learning Cycle

Study
Teachers work in collaborative planning teams (grade-level, vertical, or departmental) to examine critically and discuss the learning expectations from the selected state standards. Teachers working collaboratively develop a common understanding of • the concepts and skills students need to know and be able to do to meet the expectations in the standards, • how the standards for a grade or course are assessed on state and local tests, and • how the standards fit within the scope and sequence of the district curriculum.
Select
Collaborative planning teams research and select instructional strategies and resources for enhancing learning as described in the standards. Teachers working collaboratively • identify effective research-based strategies and appropriate resources that will be used to support learning in the selected state standards and • agree on appropriate assessment techniques that will be used to provide evidence of student learning.
Plan
Planning teams, working together, formally develop a common lesson incorporating the selected strategies and agree on the type of student work each teacher will use later (in Step 5: Analyze) as evidence of student learning. Teachers working collaboratively • develop a common formal plan outlining the lesson objectives (relevant to the standards), the materials to be used, the procedures, the time frame for the lesson, and the activities in which students will be engaged, and • decide what evidence of student learning will be collected during the implementation.
Implement
Teachers carry out the planned lesson, make note of implementation successes and challenges, and gather the agreed-upon evidence of student learning. Teachers working collaboratively • deliver the lesson as planned within the specified time period; • record results, especially noting where students struggled and/or where instruction did not achieve expected outcomes; and • collect the agreed-upon evidence of student learning to take back to the collaborative planning team.
Analyze
Teachers gather again in collaborative teams to examine student work and discuss student understanding of the standards. Teachers working collaboratively • revisit and familiarize themselves with the standards before analyzing student work; • analyze a sampling of student work for evidence of student learning; • discuss whether students have met the expectations outlined in the standards and make inferences about the strengths, weaknesses, and implications of instruction; and • identify what students know and what skills or knowledge needs to be strengthened in future lessons.

Table 5.1. The Professional Teaching and Learning Cycle *(continued)*

Adjust
Collaborative teams reflect on the implications of the analysis of student work. Teachers discuss alternative instructional strategies or modifications to the original instructional strategy that may be better suited to promoting student learning. Teachers working collaboratively   • reflect on their common or disparate teaching experiences;   • consider and identify alternative instructional strategies for future instruction;   • refine and improve the lesson; and   • determine when the instructional modifications will take place, what can be built into subsequent lessons, and what needs an additional targeted lesson.

Source: SEDL. (2008). *The professional teaching and learning cycle: Introduction.* Austin, TX: Author.

Figure 5.1. What Teachers Do in a Professional Learning Team

Review annual assessment and benchmark data

Step 1: Study
Study the standards, the concepts and skills necessary to master the standards, and how the standards are assessed

Step 2: Select
Select research-based instructional strategies and assessment techniques

Step 3: Plan
Develop a formal lesson plan, and reach agreement regarding evidence of student learning

Step 4: Implement
Deliver lesson, note successes and challenges, and collect evidence of student learning

Step 5: Analyze
Revisit the standard, analyze a sampling of student work, discuss progress toward expectations, and identify student strengths and weaknesses

Step 6: Adjust
Reflect on teaching experiences, consider alternative instructional strategies, refine and improve the lesson incorporating instructional modifications

PROFESSIONAL TEACHING AND LEARNING CYCLE

change how teachers might teach a concept to their students. Little new learning took place during these meetings. New teachers would follow along in these conversations, but they would rarely gain insight into how best to teach a concept.

Beginning the Process

The first step to move toward more meaningful and effective professional conversations and their related actions was to introduce the PTLC process to the leaders in the district in enough depth that they would be able to introduce the process to their schools. Four of the 19 schools in the district were identified as sites in which SEDL would provide extensive follow-up by working with the administrators and instructional coaches on a regular basis to help provide guidance on supporting professional learning teams during their weekly meetings. SEDL staff also sat in on professional learning teams as they met in order to provide guidance and feedback on their progress.

The principal of Low Country Middle School made it a priority that the school's instructional coach was at every professional learning team meeting and that he or his assistant principal would attend as many as possible but no fewer than three out of every four meetings. Teachers began to understand that having someone sitting in on their meetings was the new norm. The presence of the school's instructional leaders also sent a strong signal that these meetings were important and that the focus of the meeting was on instruction only. Team discussions of how many books to order changed to discussions of how the books would help teach a concept in the state standards and how the teachers would obtain evidence that students had learned the concept.

The Learning Emerged

One of the first "a-ha" moments arose when one social studies teacher was reviewing the standards and noticed a rather significant one that was not addressed in the textbook. That small, almost insignificant insight got the attention of all the social studies teachers in the school to hunt for other gaps between what they had been teaching and what was expected of the students at their grade level. Soon, that led to deeper learning conversations about how to organize their units in a way that made more sense to them than following the order outlined in the textbook. They began to really use the "Study" step of the PTLC and soon moved to having more intense dialogue about the "Select" step as they learned from one another how to teach the concepts and skills in each unit.

One member of the social studies team had to leave midyear and a new teacher, fresh from undergraduate school, joined the team. Two things occurred that don't often happen when a new teacher comes into a school. First of all, the novice teacher was able to get a clear picture of what to teach and how to teach it from the conversations he was having with his peers. Since the teachers were all exploring new ways of approaching their content, his ideas were immediately accepted and he was not forced to go through induction as a "newbie."

The next big "a-ha" happened when one teacher brought out the results of a test he had been giving his students for the past few years and asked his colleagues to help him review the results and look for trends that might uncover students' misconceptions about the content he had just taught. His colleagues examined the standards on which the unit was based and they all soon discovered that the test was not measuring students' mastery of the standards the teacher thought he was addressing. This scenario took place during the time teachers were meeting about the "Analyze" portion of the PTLC.

When teachers began to review evidence of student learning (student work), they became stymied trying to figure out how to address areas that the students hadn't yet mastered but continue to move on to their next unit so they could keep up with the scope and sequence of the curriculum. They expressed their concern to the instructional coach who was at their meeting. Since the coach had heard similar concerns from other teachers, she met with the principal to work out a solution. The principal arranged for a district consultant to come to the school to provide some on-site professional development for the teachers on differentiating instruction, so that they could learn how to expand their repertoire for addressing different levels and styles of learning.

It All Comes Together

Over time, the principal replaced all traditional staff meetings with all of the learning teams meeting together, after school in the media center. There, they had access to resources as they met and could call on the instructional coach or check with the principal about how to access professional development opportunities that would address the issues arising during their meetings. They also had immediate access to teachers at other grade levels so that conversations emerged about how skills and concepts were developed over time and across grade levels. During one vertical articulation meeting, two teams discovered a discrepancy between how a learning standard was described in the state standards documents at two different grade levels, prompting them to contact the state department about the problem.

The professional "buzz" in the media center when the teachers met was synergistic. Teachers began to take on more leadership roles and that fact became very clear when the school decided to videotape one of the afternoon sessions. The videographer stopped at each group long enough to get a grasp of the conversation and from time to time he focused on the material they were discussing. What was remarkable was that as the camera recorded the conversations, it was impossible to know at which table the principal, assistant principal, and instructional coach were sitting. Each one was simply a participant in the conversations about student learning and what the teachers leading the conversation needed to do to adjust instruction. Watching that video, there was no mistaking that the school had become a professional learning community and that the teachers had taken on a true professional orientation to their work.

Although having a structured protocol to follow during professional learning team meetings helped this school, the other two schools followed a different path toward professionalism. These three schools all took different paths to developing professional learning communities, but they all included the attributes of a PLC defined in Chapter 2 and described in the Innovation Configuration Map in Chapter 4:

- Supportive and shared leadership
- Shared values and vision
- Intentional collective learning and application of learning
- Supportive conditions (structural and relational factors)
- Shared practice

CHAPTER SIX

Turning the Finger Around

The real difficulty in changing the course of any enterprise lies not in
developing new ideas but in escaping old ones.

John Maynard Keynes

A GROUP OF TEACHERS, who had begun to work as a PLC, were
asked the question "So you've been meeting as a professional learning
community for a year and a half, what difference has it made?" One
28-year veteran teacher thought about it for a few minutes and made a gesture
and a very brief comment that sums up the change that occurs when teachers
engage wholeheartedly in a PLC. She pointed her finger toward nothing in
particular in the room and stated, "It's about turning the finger around." Her
gesture was to turn her finger from pointing off into the distance to pointing
to herself. Those few words and that small gesture symbolize the change that
occurs when teachers begin to analyze the impact that their teaching has had
on student learning. The finger no longer points at misbehaving students, dis-
engaged parents, the administration, the school board, the state department,
the legislature, or whomever has been the target of teachers' frustrations. That
teacher was acknowledging that it was her performance in the classroom that
makes the difference. She is holding herself more accountable because her
team is holding her more accountable. She has a team she can rely on to
support her as she faces the many instructional challenges facing teachers.
Changes in beliefs and values like this are not easy to come by.

With many dynamics influencing the teaching profession (history, public
perception, political agendas, economic pressures), we recognize that changing how teachers view their work and how the public perceives teaching may
be as difficult as trying to change weather patterns. However, from Chaos
Theory and the famous "Butterfly Effect" (Gleick, 1987), we also know that
small, seemingly insignificant changes can have enormous impact. For example, replacing all blown-out incandescent light bulbs with compact fluorescent
light bulbs can significantly reduce energy needs, resulting in the reduction of

greenhouse gases that can have a huge impact on climate. This small change means that we have to accept buying funny-looking light bulbs and the "we" must mean more than a few eco-conscious families; it must mean that everyone engages in the changed behavior. Over time, this small shift toward efficiency can have enormous impact on our environment.

AMPLIFYING THE IMPACT OF PLCs

These musings on the relationship between scientific principles and human behavior led to a re-reading of *Leadership and the New Science* by Margaret Wheatley, who said:

> Two forces that we have always placed in opposition to one another—freedom and order—turn out to be partners in generating viable, well-ordered, autonomous systems. If we allow autonomy at the local level, letting individuals or units be directed in their decisions by guideposts for organizational self-reference, we can achieve coherence and continuity. . . . Under certain conditions, when the system is far from equilibrium, creative individuals can have enormous impact. It is not the law of large numbers, of favorable averages, that creates change, but the presence of a lone fluctuation that gets amplified by the system. (2006, pp. 95–96)

Although Wheatley was referring to organizations, her thoughts ring true for the teaching profession. When teachers come together on at least a weekly basis to learn how their instruction has impacted student learning and look for ways to improve their performance and student learning, they engage in behavior that can have not only a significant impact on *their* performance but also on the performance of an entire school. When the behaviors associated with true professional learning communities are in place in every school, when the lone fluctuation of PLCs get amplified by the educational system, seismic shifts can occur that move teaching from a semi-profession to the level of a profession worthy of universal respect and appropriate compensation.

Some promising ideas about how to redesign and revitalize the teaching profession are explored in *Teaching 2030: What We Must Do for Our Students and Our Public Schools—Now and in the Future* (Berry et al., 2011). The book focuses on the potential for injecting new life into the teaching profession and improving how teachers are seen by the public through redesigning teacher preparation and ongoing development; restructuring how the quality and effectiveness of teaching is measured, rewarded, and compensated; and realigning the power structures between those responsible for working directly with students (teachers) and those who provide the support for teachers to be able to do their job (administrators and politicians).

Teaching 2030 suggests that in order for these seismic shifts to occur in the teaching profession, six key "change levers" (p. 171) must occur:

- *Engaging the public with a new vision for teaching and learning*–shifting the public's image of teaching from an occupation that *anyone* can do, or that truly great teachers are those few who work as individualistic heroes and heroines (like Jaime Escalante's portrayal in *Stand and Deliver* or Erin Gruwell and her *Freedom Writers*), to an image of a profession whose members work together to learn and grow.

- *Rethinking school finance so it drives new investments and partnerships*– reallocating funds to focus on areas of greatest need such as teacher development and creating partnerships with community organizations to renew the promise of making schools the center for all social services in a community.

- *Redefining preparation and licensing to ensure highly qualified and effective teachers*–convincing both the public and lawmakers that the rigor of preparation is equivalent to that of other professions; another way of raising the perception of teachers is compensation that is commensurate with the challenges of the job.

- *Cultivating working conditions that make high-needs schools "easier to staff"*– paying close attention to providing a safe and orderly environment as well as providing enough time for teachers to collaborate on solving the instructional challenges they face, and supplying the resources and continuous assistance needed for teachers to be successful.

- *Reframing accountability for transformative results*–shifting the focus on measuring the quality of a teacher or of a school from a single metric (an annual achievement test) to an accountability system that generates a fuller picture of students' abilities.

- *Transform teacher's unions into professional guilds*–replacing the idea of teacher's unions as protectors of teachers from arbitrary decisions by administrators to a league of professionals who hold one another accountable for quality instruction and high levels of student achievement.

These six levers of change interact symbiotically. In order for the public to be willing to compensate teachers at a truly professional level, teachers need to demonstrate to the public that they exhibit the qualities of a true professional: a formal preparation and certification process tied to some form of entry examination, a skill set based on a thorough understanding of the knowledge base generated by members of the profession, and a sense of moral purpose to improve oneself and the profession in service of students.

The changes suggested by the authors of *Teaching 2030* (who are almost all practicing teachers) are not easy changes to make, since they require a shift in the perception of teaching as an occupation that has a shorter day and shorter year than that worked by individuals in the business world and as a result, is not held in very high esteem. That perception, combined with the billions of dollars poured into a system that has yet to achieve its promise to the American people—a high-quality education for all students regardless of ethnicity, economic status, background, or zip code—makes changing the public's image of teaching a very daunting task. Almost every American, including legislators in Washington, DC, and statehouses, have an inside view of the teaching profession from having spent well over 2,000 days of their lives in the company of teachers. There is no exposure to other professions that compares, even if a person were to watch every TV show ever made about doctors or lawyers.

The shift has to begin somewhere. *Teaching 2030* hints that the cultural shift required is a shift from teachers who work independently and are coordinated and guided in their work by others to a community of collaborative professionals committed to continuous improvement through the learning they do together—in short, a professional learning community.

A SHIFT IN CULTURE

Roland Barth (2006) has made a bold statement about the need for this shift in culture:

> A precondition for doing anything to strengthen our practice and improve a school is the existence of a collegial culture in which professionals talk about practice, share their craft knowledge, and observe and root for the success of one another. Without these in place, *no meaningful improvement*—no staff or curriculum development, no teacher leadership, no student appraisal, no team teaching, no parent involvement, and no sustained change—*is possible.* (p. 13; emphasis added)

A case in point is a small-town elementary school in the South Carolina piedmont. A few years ago, it was the lowest-performing school of the 17 schools in the school district. Through the patience and leadership of the administrative team, the culture shifted from one where a few caring teachers were doing their best on their own and were being pressured for better performance by administration, to a culture where teachers are all accepting the responsibility for student learning and working together in professional learning teams to form a school-wide professional learning community. Administrators no longer need to direct and control the actions of teachers. Teachers are holding one another accountable by engaging in weekly conversations that go beyond tips, tricks, and techniques. They focus on what they've learned from their students' reactions to their instruction, how they can access new learning about how to improve from one another or from external professional resources, and how to implement those new ideas. They bring back to their team information about how their changed instruction works and then they repeat the cycle. The principal and assistant principal initially facilitated the meetings, but that role has been shifted to the teachers and the administrators have taken on the role of supporting the teachers by providing necessary resources and accessing additional assistance emanating from the professional learning team meetings. The teachers themselves are determining their need for growth rather than having growth plans given to them through formal evaluation processes.

The shift in culture at the school happened over time. It began with the formal leaders setting in place the processes that teachers should have taken on themselves. Initially, teachers balked at administrators taking away their planning time—their autonomy. What made the difference over time was the "calling" that these teachers felt to provide the best they could for their students. The principal brought teachers together to talk about what was important to them and supported that sense of calling. Together, they began to identify ways of working together to address the challenges of the whole school. It was shifting the power of the decisions from those in formal power to those with the power to transform what happens in the teacher/student interaction that brought about the shift in culture. A conversation with the teachers at this school told the story. They did not speak about how the principal trusted teachers with greater autonomy or how she had set high expectations (actions that she did with a clear intention to support teachers). Instead, they spoke about what they did as a professional learning community to change how they operated together. The comments they made were inspiring:

- Conversations around the school have changed—they're now all about instruction rather than what we did last weekend.
- Planning time has a new meaning. We talk about what students need, we come up with strategies, then we come back and evaluate what we did—we figure out how to improve ourselves.

- Our conversations challenge everyone—we're on the same page about what's important to teach and how to teach those skills and concepts.
- There's no more "parking lot" planning. We know what we'll be teaching every day and our lesson plans are well developed well in advance.

These teachers didn't attribute the changes to the actions of the principal. Lao Tzu, the author of the *Tao Te Ching*, states the concept succinctly: "A leader is best when people barely know he exists, when his work is done, his aim fulfilled, they will say: we did it ourselves."

Although this school has not yet reached its full potential, it has made significant progress and has gained recognition in the community as a school that's making a difference. It may take a few more years before the community fully understands that it was how teachers worked together that made the difference for the school, but the idea of teachers taking charge of their professional growth is a beginning. It became very clear that the teachers at this school have made the shift from being isolated educational entrepreneurs to being a community of professionals who strive to improve their own learning and the learning of all students in the school. They are truly a PROFESSIONAL learning community.

Unfortunately, the attitudes and behaviors of teachers in most schools are still being shaped by the rules and regulations demanded by those outside the classroom with the power to control. If teachers are ever to become professional, they must take back the profession by negating the need for strong external supervision. The words of Parker Palmer (2007) ring true:

> The extent to which institutions control our lives depends on our own inner calculus about what we value most . . . institutions are us. . . . If institutions are rigid, it is because we fear change. If institutions are competitive, it is because we value winning over all else. If institutions are heedless of human need, it is because something in us is heedless as well. (p. 206)

Part of what's keeping teaching from being considered a valued profession by the public is that teachers are fearful of taking charge of the changes that can make the most difference for them. They need to heed the promise that professional learning communities provide—that they can take back control of the profession by having ongoing professional conversations that matter. These are conversations that focus on the value of learning and growing so that teachers "turn the finger around" and take full responsibility for student learning.

The setting for these conversations, as we have been recommending, is the professional learning community. But these settings require conditions that support the conversations and the activities of the PLC members. These conditions are of two types: structural or physical conditions, and human or relational factors. They are the subject of attention in the next two chapters.

Structures, Schedules, and Other Necessary Stuff: Creating or Reframing Professional Learning Communities

It takes nine months to make a baby, no matter how many people you put on the job.

American saying

WHETHER LAUNCHING A NEW PLC or restructuring an existing one to raise its level of professional direction and function, it is essential to prepare logistical/structural factors for the PLC prior to engaging in its processes and learning. Identifying and describing action for these required preparations is the goal of this chapter. Having identified and described these factors, a variety of ways that PLCs have been successfully initiated will be shared.

It is obvious that time to meet and a place for doing so are primary considerations for preparing to launch a PLC. School after school reports to us that it is nigh impossible to find or create the time for the community to meet. This chapter will address this knotty problem as well as other structural issues and schedules. In addition, we will examine material resources for the learning of the community, and also, the human resources necessary for study and learning. The development and use of organizational structures such as a variety of communication systems will also be given attention.

TIME AND SPACE

Time to meet is probably the most challenging of all factors for the initiation of a PLC. While many schools have been troubled and severely challenged by this requirement, others have solved the dilemma in a variety of ways.

Time

Many schools in many districts now have a work schedule that provides time each day for planning, assessing student work, conducting conferences with parents, and convening meetings with grade-level or subject-matter colleagues. In many districts, the time for such activities is designated once a week for meeting with colleagues in a learning community, where participants engage in their professional learning activities.

In other circumstances, time is much more difficult to find or create. Some schools have solved this problem by delaying the opening of the school day, so that teachers and administrators can meet for 45 minutes to an hour. Others encourage staff to remain after the typical day, supporting this additional time through serving participants an early dinner provided by a community business. Several innovative schools have found the means by which to extend the regular school day's instruction for 20 minutes, 4 days of the week. Then, adjourning and dismissing students early on the 5th day of the week provides the staff an hour and a half to meet for community learning work. This schema, of course, requires working with any transportation schedules and with school parents who understand the benefits to their children when teachers learn and become more effective in their roles.

Still other schools have found a way to release teachers from their classroom duties through the use of "specials"—when students attend a music, art, physical education, or media/library class. The specials schedule rotates so that one or two grade levels of students, or academic subject groups, can attend together. It does not provide for the entire faculty to meet as a community. Other schools have engaged the participation of reliable and (modestly) trained parents to release the classroom teacher, who provides the plan that the parent follows with the students. Another district that we know prepared lesson packets for the parent/substitute to follow. These packets were designed for enrichment activities, and although they added meaningfully to the academic experiences of the students, they did not attempt to represent the sequence of lessons embedded in the curriculum. Other possibilities from Hord and Sommers (2008, pp. 56–57) include adding minutes to the beginning and end of 4 days of the week, then dismissing students after lunch on Friday so teachers can meet; extending the school year to gain days when the students are not present; extending to 8-hour workdays so that staff meets after students are dismissed; having staff arrive an hour earlier in the day or remain an hour after the day for meeting; scheduling meetings on Saturdays (some schools pay an honorarium for this to teachers); using scheduled faculty meetings for professional learning communities; and using stipends from grants to pay for teachers' release time.

Space

Many schools have exceeded the number of students expected to attend in the current facility. This has caused space such as libraries and auditoriums to be "converted" to accommodate classrooms. It has also resulted in challenges for finding space for staff to meet. One learning community found that it could use the auditorium stage after the lunch hour. Another used a part of the cafeteria, again after the lunch hour. One high school that used the cafeteria made a related service project for students, who efficiently brought the cafeteria to a clean and "orderly" status, so that various teacher groups could meet soon thereafter.

In one interesting solution to the space problem, where there was no regularly available space for meeting, the principal persuaded the staff to meet in the teachers' classrooms, rotating around the building and into all classrooms on an arranged schedule. Teachers selected the date for which their classroom would be used. This arrangement not only provided space, but it also gave teachers an opportunity to be inside classrooms and to have a "peek" at the learning agenda in the classroom through learning materials exhibited on bulletin boards and displays of student work on library tables. In this way, teachers became better acquainted with one another. As a result, one of the 5th-grade teachers noticed a "word wall" example in a primary classroom, and asked the 2nd-grade teacher if she could return for further examination and explanation. This request raised the 2nd-grade teacher's professional self-esteem, as he gained stature in the eyes of his upper-grade colleagues. This example demonstrates an added benefit to meeting in teachers' classrooms, even if individuals' chins touch their knees in the kindergarten rooms.

Another innovative example of solving the space problem occurred on an extremely large, and overpopulated, middle school campus. This campus housed multiple buildings and teachers were distributed widely across it. The administrative team gave each of the teachers a blueprint of the campus and all the buildings, and a schedule of when the academic subject-matter learning communities had requested to meet. Accompanying these materials was a challenge to the academic subject-matter teams to organize themselves and decide where each of the learning teams could meet regularly, at the time they had designated earlier. This enabled the teams to select locations and check with other teams to ensure that the location wasn't already "spoken" for. The administrators characterized the activity as a "Scavenger Hunt" and initiated it with a hot dog roast. It's interesting what a few sausages can do to stimulate collegial interaction and problem solving. It's also interesting how the administrators giving teachers this small opportunity for decision-making elevated the treatment of staff as professionals.

COMMUNICATION STRUCTURES

Many schools have organized professional learning communities as grade-level or academic department teams. Such small teams as communities of learning are extremely practical, for they provide opportunities to focus on a particular academic subject area, or on the specific needs of students in a particular grade. We endorse these learning teams, and strongly urge, in addition, the creation of a whole faculty community. In each case, communication becomes an imperative so that the school has common goals, as well as smaller unit outcomes. Practical and efficient means for sharing and interaction can contribute immeasurably to the developing professionalism of the faculty.

Meetings

The weekly faculty meeting was typically a time for sharing information. In many buildings, this meeting still exists wherein the administrator generally reports a list of "what to dos" and "what not to dos" that emanates from district office or from the principal's office. There may be some discussion of topics specific to the particular school, such as when the Science Fair will be scheduled, who will head committees, and so forth. Not very often does this meeting serve any purpose other than to share information, or to gather information, preferences, or suggestions from the staff—and its current purpose could be served through paper or electronic media, freeing this time for staff study and learning.

Email Messages

In many buildings, the old-style faculty meeting no longer exists as learning communities and other activities have superseded its place on the schedule. Most schools have computers, if not in every classroom, most certainly on every teacher's desk. Information messages can be easily and immediately delivered to each staff member in the building. Responses can be solicited from the staff, so that some interaction is conducted. Communicating in this way is dependent on every individual reviewing his/her electronically conveyed messages routinely, and in a timely fashion.

Staff Mailboxes

Despite the presence of computers throughout many buildings, staff mailboxes in the central office of the school appear to remain as another avenue of information flow. In these, deposits of paper-based information from the central office may be placed. Articles and periodicals delivered by the U.S. Postal Service may also be routed to individuals, teams, or whole faculty lists through staff boxes.

Newsletters

Weekly or semi-weekly newsletters have been frequent devices used by many schools to communicate with staff, with parents, and other school community-based persons. Although some principals may use this means to communicate almost daily with teachers, the larger majority appear to be using paperless technology to do this. Even graphs and charts, data tables, and pictorial material can be conveyed through the staffs' computers, making paper newsletters much less frequent "communicators."

Electronic Networking

Many of the previous methods of communications are rapidly being replaced by the electronic versions of communication that make email appear as antiquated as "snail mail." Professional organizations as well as school districts have registered on social networking sites although, ironically, many of those same institutions block Internet access to those same sites. Texting has become ubiquitous in many circles, and new teachers often communicate with one another in this manner. One of the most useful forms of networking is the availability for teachers simultaneously to share and edit documents and resources through remote servers. They do this through attachments to email, through membership in various websites, and through other electronic mechanisms (refer to your local technology guru for local possibilities).

MATERIAL RESOURCES

So that PLCs can support teachers in increasing their professional practice, most certainly professional materials must be available for the individual and the communities' studies and learning. These materials will include relevant journals for the levels of the school, and for the various academic disciplines. CDs and DVDs are abundant from many publishers and educational enterprises. Further, much material is easily found on the Internet, so that connectivity is essential.

Many school libraries/media centers house a professional section. Here, professional books, journals, articles clipped by the librarian and/or teachers, and conference take-home materials may be found. Keeping them organized for ready reference is another requirement so that these resources can be readily used. Most media specialists (librarians) have been trained for this, so their assistance should be solicited.

HUMAN RESOURCES

Because the PLC purpose and reason for existence is its members' continuous professional learning as it relates to their students' needs for successful learning, part of the "Necessary Stuff" will be access to consultants and other experts when needed. Most certainly, the community turns to its members for advice, counsel, and learning about how to teach in order to gain specific results. If such expertise does not reside within the community, then other communities across the school may be canvassed in a solicitation for help. If this exploration does not prove fruitful, the search may extend to other schools, and/or to the district office. If the outcomes of this search are not successful, then efforts may be directed to an intermediate service center, the state department of education, or to an independent consultant who has the knowledge, skills, and talents for the challenge.

Such was the case when several PLCs in a school district learned about a new state mathematics standard. The teachers thought that the standard was a wise addition to their grade-level students' learning outcomes, but when they considered it further, they couldn't identify anyone in their PLCs or on their staffs who knew how to teach this standard for students' learning. They queried colleagues in other schools, then asked district office personnel to help them. Finally, the school administrators engaged in a search for a state or national consultant who could work with the teachers so that they could learn an approach and strategies for teaching the new standard successfully to their students. Sometimes, the circle must widen to find the resources needed for new community learning.

INITIATING THE PROFESSIONAL LEARNING COMMUNITY

Once logistical and organizational preparations for creating or re-professionalizing a PLC have established the "foundation and framing," the next step is to examine how a PLC might be initiated.

We have seen multiple examples of the initiation of communities of professional learners. For the most part, these have been mobilized by principals or other school leaders in the building. How they have catalyzed staff to become communities of professional learners has been quite varied, as we shall see.

A Rural High School

In the mid-1990s, for example, in a small-town comprehensive high school in Oklahoma, the principal was quite interested in bringing the faculty together to determine where they needed to focus learning for themselves. However, he was very uncertain how to initiate the gathering of the teachers, when an ideal opportunity fell onto his desk. The school board requested his opinion on whether they should create a policy to require a uniform dress code for the students.

He called a meeting of the faculty, presented the request, and invited responses. After multiple suggestions and 35 minutes of interactions, he offered his thanks for their willing remarks, but also commented that all suggestions appeared to be opinions—which was not a bad thing—but perhaps it would be wise to be able to offer the board some ideas that had some supportive evidence. And perhaps it would also be wise to broaden their sphere of inquiry to discover what the students, parents, and community members thought about the issue.

These comments resulted in the teachers identifying several committees, in which all the teachers would participate, to do some investigative work to learn what the broader school population thought about the issue of student uniforms—a sensitive topic in this area of the state. Thus, committees were charged to learn what students, parents, and community business members thought, and to explore the research to ascertain if other high schools had reported experience with uniforms and their success or lack of same. Everyone was requested to discover, if possible, any evidence that would suggest any kind of direct impact on student learning outcomes, as a result of a policy enforcing a student uniform. The educators agreed to return in 2 weeks to meet and report what they had learned.

The principal heaved a sigh of relief that his yet ill-defined plan to engage the staff in learning had taken the first step: The entire faculty had agreed to undertake a learning activity together.

When the staff convened as planned, the reports were met with expressions of surprise and some concern, especially the report of the parents' reactions, which showed that parents were concerned about the expenses of such a new policy on their children's clothing budgets. The staff decided that they did not have sufficient information to make a recommendation to the board, because they had gained no information or evidence about how uniform clothing impacts student learning and behavior. Thus, they decided that they should research the experiences of other schools that had instituted such a policy to learn about how the policy influenced students. They organized for this endeavor with the head librarian's help in locating such schools or districts, and departed with the promise of returning in 2 weeks with their additional learning.

The staff created a report for the board that was made with full disclosure about the staff's exploration process, and the conclusions about uniforms for the students that came from their investigation. Except for an outlet store that was quite willing to handle purchases of the uniforms, all other entities examined for their opinions or preferences were negative. Three high schools that had experienced the use of a uniform dress code reported that the "new attire" in their schools did not in any way enhance academic learning or improve social behaviors.

Although some of the staff thought that this activity had been "much ado about nothing," the significance of this first-ever activity of the staff, collaborating to learn about a topic of importance, was its collegial learning. The principal congratulated the faculty for their learning process and the results that they had obtained. Before he dismissed them, he provided each educator with a brief text, a summary of the school-wide student achievement scores that had arrived 3 days previously, with an invitation to come together to examine the data the following week. It was reasonably clear that the principal would continue to direct the faculty on a learning journey, stimulated by student data that indicated where their performance was poor (as you might guess, the principal had already reviewed the data and learned what they contained). His ultimate goal was to acquaint staff with data and their use in focusing staff on their own learning—as a means for improving their teaching for students. He would guide the staff until they were ready to steer themselves and organize into self-directed adult learning teams.

A K–8 School

This school in the arid desert region of New Mexico was located on the fringe of a small city, and was the focus of an early 1990 research study on administrator-teacher collaboration. The school had a high percentage population of Hispanic students, many of whom were second-language learners. The teachers and the single administrator had been expressing concern about the poor mathematics performance of their students, and gathered early in the fall semester to discuss their students' work.

As they lamented about the outcomes that were being produced by students, the principal invited suggestions about what might be addressed to improve student results. The group brainstormed, creating a list of four possibilities:

- parent disinterest and lack of participation in their students' learning;
- health and well-being of the students;
- mathematics instruction—curriculum and instructional strategies;
- staff stress and lack of energy.

A rather lengthy discussion of each of these factors elicited more uncertainty and frustration by the faculty. The principal suggested that they organize into four "research teams" to study each of the factors to learn what the issues surrounding each factor might be, and what might be done to correct it. Because this principal routinely invited teachers into problem solving, giving them ownership of the problem and the possibilities of solving the problem, they were accustomed to investigating issues. Teachers across all grade levels volunteered for the factor of their interest, met with their factor's team, and made plans for what they would do.

Ten days later, they met to discuss their findings. "What did you learn, and consequently, what do you suggest?" queried the principal. Each of the four teams reported, some more fully than others. The item about which there was more precise and significant data was how curriculum and instruction related to the low performance of the students in mathematics. This team had studied the math achievement scores of all grade levels, had visited math classrooms, talked with the teachers about their mathematics instruction, and subsequently conducted a conversation with their regional laboratory personnel about what they had learned.

The mathematics instruction report was deemed to present the most promising path for improving student performance, and the teachers agreed to invite the regional lab people to come to discuss what might be done, and what the faculty would have to learn and how they would learn it . . . all in the spirit of improving the performance of their students.

The principal was delighted, for, as she commented to the faculty, the math instruction was a factor over which they had control, and could take action. Further, she congratulated them on their searches and their learning that had accrued, noting that she expected further learning from them about mathematics and how to improve their math teaching for students.

A Middle School

A small middle school in rural South Carolina has found ways to form a variety of learning teams to create a school-wide community of professional learners. In the early stages of the development of PLCs, the school had teachers who taught the same content at the same grade level meeting together. Initially, that consisted of small groups of two or three teachers meeting with the instructional coach on a weekly basis. After some budget cuts that impacted the school for 2 years, the numbers of teachers in those small teams was reduced even further and in some cases there was only one teacher per grade level teaching a core content area. The principal then helped the teachers set up times when the entire grade level, teachers of all disciplines, could come together to learn from one another about strategies for writing across content areas or the development of open-ended response items to assess student learning. A need then arose for teachers teaching the same content to have an opportunity to share and learn together, so a third type of learning team was formed–of vertical teams across grade levels teaching the same content.

This third type of learning team focused on having members bring, to all meetings, evidence of student learning in the form of student class work (writing, responses to open-ended response items, and so on). That led the school's leadership team to develop a fourth type of learning team. Once a month after school, six teachers (most often from different content area teams) each volunteered to bring in 4 to 5 samples of student work, representing a range of quality, the relevant state standards, and the assignment that led to that student work. They prepared six copies of all materials for sharing in small groups.

The entire faculty now meets in the school's media center and as teachers arrive they are assigned to one of the tables where the volunteers are seated. At one table, a 6th-grade math teacher may be presenting student work and the expectations for student learning from the standards to a 7th-grade science teacher, an 8th-grade language arts teacher, a special education teacher, a music teacher, and the assistant principal. The four types of professional conversations about teaching and learning have had an incredible effect on the school. Rather than dreading multiple meetings, teachers are seeing the connections that exist across content areas and across grade levels. They are working together as a whole-school professional learning community to take mutual responsibility for the learning of all students as well as setting high expectations for one another as professionals who are continuously learning more effective ways to meet the needs of all students.

LEARNING ABOUT LAUNCHING

The three stories of the schools have a common factor: In each case, the principal made certain that the community had a purpose or reason to engage in their own learning, as an initial step. By the time the elementary school's PLC developed, the educational literature was beginning to contain research studies about PLC. These early research efforts resulted in descriptive findings that described the PLC's actions. There remained much to learn about how to really create such a community of professional learners, how to support its productivity and to maintain its continuous learning and work. What became clear, however, was the importance of the relationships that could or should be nurtured within and across the members of the community. That is the topic of the next chapter.

CHAPTER EIGHT

Relationships: The Soul of Professional Learning Communities

One incontrovertible finding emerges from my career spent working in and around schools: the nature of relationships among the adults within a school has a greater influence on the character and quality of that school and on student accomplishment than anything else.

Roland Barth (2006)

AT AN ELEMENTARY SCHOOL, teachers were just beginning to look together at student work. They were encouraged to bring samples of student work from a lesson that they had previously explained to the team. They came to a grade-level meeting to discuss the evidence of student learning they saw in the work. The teacher sharing the student work began to feel very defensive as the other teachers honestly described the degree to which the samples showed or did not show attainment of the expectations in the standards, and grade-level expectations used to plan the lesson. As the conversation progressed, the teacher grew more and more anxious, and before the meeting was over, she left the room in tears.

At another school, a similar scenario unfolded but with a very different result. As the team of teachers analyzed the student work samples, the teacher who had presented the work had an "aha" moment when she realized that the assignment and resulting work samples had little connection to the learning expectations in the standard she had focused on to design the lesson. She thanked her colleagues for helping her think through the results of her teaching, and together with her team, devised a new strategy to teach the concept and assess student understanding of the concept more effectively.

There may be many reasons that these two teachers reacted in two different ways, but the fact that the second scenario took place in the same

South Carolina school that was described in Chapter 6 should be no surprise. The fact remains that when teachers engage in authentic conversation about the relationship between their teaching and students' learning, it is a very personal experience. In a PLC, teaching becomes a public act, not something that occurs behind a closed door. Teachers' knowledge of content and their skill with implementing effective instructional strategies are open to the scrutiny of their fellow teachers, for better or worse. A school climate that supports open, trusting relationships creates a context in which teachers can collaborate without feeling great personal risk—the risk of feeling judged by their peers to be less than adequate. It's easy to say but difficult to achieve.

THE ROLE OF TRUST

The foundation of a positive school climate is the development of trust between teachers and administrators and among teachers themselves. Parker Palmer (2007) describes the challenge of creating a culture of trust—the root of the problem is fear. Truth be told, many teachers live with fear on a daily basis. For some, it may be a fear of physical danger in a school where students are undisciplined and unruly; in hard economic times, it may be fear of losing a job. But, for most, the fears they face are more subtle. Teachers fear that they may not be able to engage and motivate students, especially those students whose lives are vastly different from theirs—lives full of poverty, violence, drug or alcohol abuse. They fear that administrators, fellow teachers, parents, and worse yet, students, will judge them for being inadequate teachers. Their greatest fear may be that they may have to change much of what they believe about what constitutes good teaching. When teachers behave as true professionals, they work through the fear and "turn the finger around," no longer putting the blame of failure to learn on the students, but looking deeply at their own *actions* and how they contribute to the *reactions* they receive from students. The way to overcome fear is to face it head on, but that often requires having the support of trusted peers.

Palmer (2007) tells the story of a shop teacher whose principal had been urging him to attend a summer institute on technology so that the students wouldn't be tied to outdated procedures. The teacher refused to go, stating that it was more important for the students to learn the basics of the craft's techniques and that they could pick up the refinements later. At the same time, the teacher was involved in a series of *Courage to Teach* weekend retreats (a form of professional learning community) with Palmer, and he was engaged with fellow teachers in deep reflection about who they are as teachers and what they value the most about their profession. As a result, the teacher was able to admit that he was afraid that he wouldn't understand how to apply the technology and that his field was passing him by.

That admission opened a dialogue between them and the teacher and the principal attended the institute together. Facing his fear, being honest with his need for improvement, and being willing to change marked a shift in the level of professionalism for that teacher, but it took a great deal of courage and trust that he would not be harshly judged by his principal. Having the support of a group of colleagues in whom he could confide and whom he trusted provided the teacher with the support he needed to be open about his fear.

Trust is the foundation on which teachers can be open and honest enough to collaborate and develop a sense of collective efficacy (Goddard, Hoy, & Woolfolk Hoy, 2000). That sense of collective efficacy is positively associated with student achievement (Bandura, 1993; Goddard, Hoy, & Woolfolk Hoy, 2000). When teachers at a school develop an attitude that says "as a team we can really make a difference for students no matter what they bring to the table," it develops a culture of openness and trust that is the foundation for PLCs. That raises the question of how to achieve a level of trust that overcomes the fear of exposing your teaching habits to others, and thereby develop a culture of collective efficacy.

Megan Tschannen-Moran, in her book *Trust Matters: Leadership for Successful Schools* (2004), summarizes her many years of research on the topic of trust. She describes the qualities that leaders must possess and the associated behaviors that develop a culture of trust in a school:

Benevolence: Caring, extending good will, having positive intentions, supporting teachers, expressing appreciation for staff efforts, being fair, guarding confidential information

Honesty: Having integrity, telling the truth, keeping promises, honoring agreements, having authenticity, accepting responsibility, avoiding manipulation, being real, being true to oneself

Openness: Engaging in open communication, sharing important information, delegating, sharing decision-making, sharing power

Reliability: Having consistency, being dependable, demonstrating commitment, having dedication, being diligent

Competence: Setting an example, engaging in problem solving, fostering conflict resolution (rather than avoidance), working hard, pressing for results, setting standards, buffering teachers, handling difficult situations, being flexible. (p. 34)

FOUR FACETS OF TRUST

These facets of trust rarely occur in isolation, and when an individual is acting in a way that engenders trust, he or she is most likely demonstrating two or three of the five facets in all encounters with colleagues. A few scenarios from schools in which we've worked can help paint a picture of what the development of trust looks like in action.

A Principal

While she demonstrates care during personal crises and creates celebrations to appreciate teachers, one high school principal is really communicating positive intentions (benevolence). We've heard this idea communicated by teachers in comments such as "Our principal really supports us—she has our back." That statement is not just about supporting the teachers as they face unruly students or have to deal with uncooperative parents. The principal of this school makes sure that teachers know that she will protect the time that teachers have to work together, even when she has to stand up to the central office and say "no" to their requests to pull teachers for some training that doesn't align with the school's goals (reliability, competence).

She is good-natured and is in constant touch with her teachers in classrooms, hallways, lunchtime, and before and after school (openness), asking them very sincerely how things are going and how can she support them (benevolence, reliability). If a teacher is experiencing some personal stress, she'll set aside time to make sure that he receives the support he needs from fellow teachers and from the school's instructional coach (benevolence, reliability). She sets an example within the school about caring for students and caring for the adults (benevolence, competence). She also makes it a priority to let teachers know that she holds them in high regard, and when they demonstrate professionalism, she defers more often to their professional judgment (honesty, competence).

A Superintendent

A small-town superintendent we know begins each year by inviting all new teachers to his home the day before they report to work and takes the time to get to know each individual (benevolence, openness). The message he is sending about caring for teachers would seem like an empty gesture if that same level of connection didn't carry forward throughout the school year (benevolence, reliability). He appreciates the fact that teachers need to feel and experience competence as they go about their job and that feeling of efficacy will pay off in their attitude and level of energy as they face the daily challenges of teaching and learning (benevolence, competence). Trust begins with those in formal leadership positions but as it permeates an organization, teachers tend to provide the same level of trust and support for one another in their professional learning communities.

An Instructional Coach

Moving from being a fellow teacher to the position of instructional coach in the same building can present a challenge for both the teachers in the school and the new instructional coach. In one such school, the coach spent her first few months establishing trust in this new relationship by acknowledging the change while continuing to be the same genuine person she had been with the teachers on her team (honesty, openness, reliability). She was able to communicate that sense of authenticity with the teachers she hadn't worked closely with before, and within less than a year she had developed a trusting relationship with all of the teachers in the school. They knew that her intentions were always positive and that she would never betray personal information (benevolence, reliability). She also made sure to provide teachers with information she received from meetings at the central office (openness) and followed through with accessing resources for teachers as soon as they needed them (honesty and reliability).

An Assistant Principal

A young assistant principal was having a difficult time with a team of middle school teachers who were much more experienced and had little respect for his contributions to their team meetings. When the social studies teacher had to leave school to tend to an emergency at home, the assistant principal took over the class and didn't miss a beat with the planned lesson, even though his teaching experience was at an elementary school (benevolence, reliability, competence). The entire team took notice of the ease with which he handled the content and the students. When the social studies teacher returned, the difference in age between the assistant principal and the team members no longer mattered. He had demonstrated his competence as a teacher and gained the trust of the team who now easily included him in their instructional deliberations (openness, reliability, competence).

There is no magic bullet to create the conditions in which teachers feel safe enough to share deeply and openly with their colleagues about the challenges they face in their classroom. There are three qualities, though, that are essential to developing a climate of trust in a school–authenticity, consistency, and persistence, all qualities of a consummate professional. There are few approaches used in schools or in teacher or administrator preparation programs that address those qualities. The *Courage to Teach* is an example of a program that helps teachers access their authentic voices and develop a sense of resilience in this demanding profession. Teachers come together to dialogue about the personal and professional issues that constitute their life in schools. They have the opportunity to engage in deep reflection about their vocation as a professional while rediscovering the joys related to working with young minds. Most important, teachers develop the openness and trust that are so necessary to the success of a professional learning community.

Whatever the path of renewal, when teachers meet in safe spaces to share openly and move beyond fears of judgment, it helps teachers get back in touch with their calling as professional educators. In supportive communities of colleagues, they learn to listen deeply to their fellow teachers and that transfers to their ability to hear what their students are telling them. They hear what their students are telling them by way of their actions, through their writing, and through the many forms of nonverbal communication that always speak louder than words. When teachers have experienced hearing others and being heard in a profound way, they develop the skills to be effective listeners, and that quality helps them connect with their students–students who are more willing to learn from someone who truly hears them.

One reliable indicator of success is student response. When students say things like "One of the most important aspects of high schools is that teachers care and be willing to change to become better teachers," there is a PLC that is having an impact. Teachers don't become caring through legislation or going to a one-shot workshop. By demonstrating care for their students, they exhibit the human qualities that make great teachers and great professionals.

In a study of the *Courage to Teach* program, McMahon (2003) suggests that in order to sustain a passion for teaching–in other words, the commitment, resilience, and sense of efficacy necessary to engage in the profession–teachers had to find ways to decrease the elements that exhaust their energy (a culture of isolation, lack of respect for the profession, heavy workloads) and find ways to remain energized. She noted that teachers in her study renewed their energy through personal reflection about their effectiveness as a teacher and by having caring, supportive, professional relationships at school.

In a later study, Poutiatine (2005) promotes the following attitudes and dispositions:

- capacity for collegial relationships in the workplace (both in terms of skills in building these relationships and motivation toward building these relationships);
- trust capacity in both self and in colleagues;
- vocational and personal clarity; and,
- self-acceptance, sense of efficacy, and courage in their professional lives.

Development of a school culture that supports the introduction, development, and maturation of professional learning communities is crucial to the work of PLCs as they engage in the Professional Teaching and Learning Cycle (see Chapter 5). The relationship between the PTLC and the surround of supporting conditions and administrative supports can be seen visually in Figure 8.1 (p. 94).

SUPPORTIVE CONDITIONS FOR PROFESSIONAL LEARNING

The context for change (the large circle) is the container in which the work of professional learning teams takes place. That container is crafted initially through the intentional efforts of school administrators and teacher leaders who, acting as servant leaders, co-create a vision that fosters professional learning, provides the structural (time, space) and instructional support needed, and offers a balance of continuous pressure and support. The favorable conditions that are created sustain the collaborative work of teachers as they engage in the work of professional learning communities.

The model also demonstrates that it's very possible to turn random acts of professional development into a coherent set of activities by providing professional learning communities with new information about content, instructional strategies, and authentic processes for monitoring student learning (the arrows pointing in to the circle). As teachers engage in professional learning communities, they also pinpoint the need for further learning through professional development focused specifically on those needs (the arrows pointing out). By determining their own needs for additional professional learning, teachers are taking charge of another area that has often been determined by others. In this way, they are taking greater control over their professional lives.

Teachers who are seeking to become true professionals know the importance of relationship. They also know its meaning: two or more individuals who feel safe enough to be open and honest, to be our true selves, with one

Figure 8.1. Context of Favorable Conditions

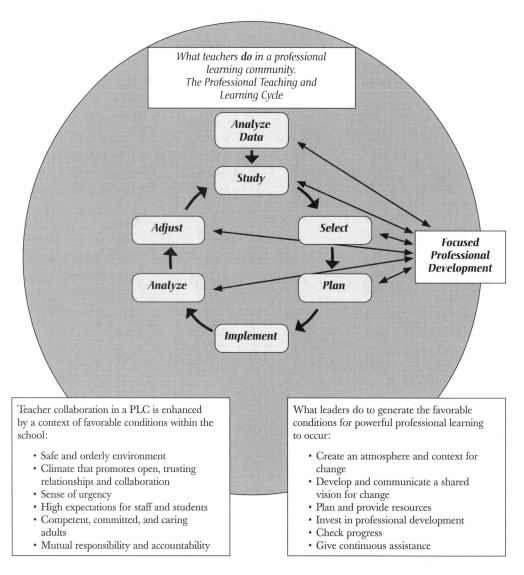

*What teachers **do** in a professional learning community. The Professional Teaching and Learning Cycle*

Analyze Data

Study

Adjust   Select

Analyze   Plan

Implement

Focused Professional Development

Teacher collaboration in a PLC is enhanced by a context of favorable conditions within the school:

- Safe and orderly environment
- Climate that promotes open, trusting relationships and collaboration
- Sense of urgency
- High expectations for staff and students
- Competent, committed, and caring adults
- Mutual responsibility and accountability

What leaders do to generate the favorable conditions for powerful professional learning to occur:

- Create an atmosphere and context for change
- Develop and communicate a shared vision for change
- Plan and provide resources
- Invest in professional development
- Check progress
- Give continuous assistance

Source: Adapted from Tobia, E. (2007). The Professional Teaching and Learning Cycle: Implementing a standards-based approach to professional development. *SEDL Letter, 19*(1), 11–15.

another. Parker Palmer knows that relationships are fundamentally a form of mutual respect that is often called unconditional love:

> The people who help us grow toward true self offer unconditional love, neither judging us to be deficient nor trying to force us to change but accepting us exactly as we are. And yet this unconditional love does not lead us to rest on our laurels. Instead, it surrounds us with a charged force field that makes us want to grow from the inside out—a force field that is safe enough to take the risks and endure the failures that growth requires. (2004, p. 47)

In the workplace, discussions of unconditional love seem less than professional. However, the underlying concept conveys an important message: When we can support one another without judgment—i.e., without conditions—we open the door to the kinds of trusting relationships in schools that encourage professionalism.

CHAPTER NINE

And Yet . . . Becoming a True Professional

> To improve is to change; to change is to learn;
> to learn is to create oneself endlessly.
>
> adapted from Henri Bergson (1859–1941)

A S THE BERGSON QUOTE ABOVE SUGGESTS, there can be no improvement without change, and no change without learning. Change *is* learning; it's as simple and as complicated as that (Hall & Hord, 2011). And, what we know of professionals is that they are continuous learners, always changing in order to improve their practice and to serve their clients more effectively.

We have been exploring the professional learning community structure and strategy as a means for reaching the goal—that of developing educational practitioners as true professionals. In previous chapters, we have provided ideas and information that explain and exemplify the "supportive conditions" required of an effective PLC: structural supports in Chapter 7, and human and relational resources in Chapter 8. There is, of course, the potential risk that teachers meet in PLCs on a regular basis, plan actions for teaching and learning, implement part of these plans in their classroom practice, but are not meeting the expectations that are set for professionals, individuals who:

- have engaged in a rigorous preparation program, and have achieved a degree of certification required of professional educators, possessing both the knowledge and skills necessary to meet the needs of all students; and
- have a strong sense of calling and a professional orientation to their work that includes a commitment to serving, in a high-quality way, *all* of the students in their schools and a commitment to collaborative, continuous learning and improvement.

In this concluding chapter, we revisit the three stories (in Chapter 5) that represent

1. the dimensions or components of effective PLCs, and
2. the actions they are taking toward increasing their students' achievement and their own collective efficacy, moving toward a professional demeanor.

THE COMMUNITY'S WORK AND PROFESSIONALISM

How do the stories of these three schools (reported in Chapter 5) characterize them as research-informed professional learning communities, focused on improving instruction—that is, the quality of their teaching that will benefit students—and, subsequently, contribute to increasing their staff's professional perspective and demeanor, as well as the posture and presence they project as professionals to their peers and the public?

Initiating a PLC

The three schools discussed earlier can be analyzed and compared to determine the varying levels of progression or degrees to which they constitute professional learning communities (see Table 9.1, pp. 98–100), using the six descriptors developed from research on PLCs (Boyd & Hord, 1994; Hall & Hord, 2011, pp. 26–28; Hipp & Huffman, 2010, p. 13; Hord, 2004, p. 7). By looking at them against this rubric, we can better answer the question: What do professionals do as a professional learning community? These key descriptors constitute the rubric for this analysis:

- Articulation of a shared vision for improvement
- Shared and supportive leadership
- Intentional collective learning
- Structural conditions
- Relational conditions
- Peers' shared practices

*A **shared vision** of improvement.* From the descriptions of these three schools in Table 9.1, it is clear that High Plains School has had considerable experience in grade-level team meetings where they have discussed instructional practice, conducted powerful conversations about their students and their work, debated frequently about professional practice, and have gained considerable comfort and ease in doing so. The members have the requisite skills for examining student data in order to employ it in instructional

text continues on p. 100

Table 9.1. How the Schools Exemplify a Community of Professional Learners

High Plains	Desert River	Low Country
Articulate a Shared Vision		
High Plains' 1st-grade team, "after weeks of study and several meetings," adopted a writing program whose goals matched those that they wished for their students. These goals became the vision toward which they planned to work.	Desert River's staff members were stalemated but were given a clear and focused set of descriptions, explanations, and expectations by their administrative team that spelled out what they would be doing in their classrooms. This served as their vision.	The leadership at Low Country initially set the expectations for how teachers would work and learn together and when teachers came together in small groups in the same room, a norm of collaborative learning was established and a shared vision emerged.
Shared and Supportive Leadership		
For 3 years, the staff members at High Plains had been given grade-level meeting time and were experienced in interacting with one another. The 1st-grade team shared decision-making and other forms of authority with one another as they did their community work and learning.	After the new approach to teaching reading settled in, each department began "working together creatively to plan their week's lessons," sharing ideas with one another and, in general, supporting one another's leadership of the group for various activities.	The principal and instructional coach helped to organize the team meetings but the teachers set their own norms for working together and took over the responsibility for facilitating all of the meetings. It was soon impossible to tell the difference between teachers and the formal leaders by their behavior in the meetings.
Structural Conditions		
The principal arranged a schedule of time for the teams in the school to meet. In addition, resources of books and other materials were provided and the principal visited the team meetings at random, but also on request of the team. The team determined in which member's room they would meet, and made requests to satisfy other needs.	The principal constructed the schedule for the new, daily reading class, as well as "checking to ensure that all department teachers had common meeting times available." All staff members were provided with all materials for their new program, and times for staff's professional learning were displayed, as well as when the reading specialist was available.	Time was established during the day for small teams to meet and traditional afterschool staff meetings were transformed into additional opportunities for teachers to share their challenges and successes and learn from one another. The afterschool time also became an opportunity for addressing common needs for new information, i.e., differentiated instruction.

Table 9.1. How the Schools Exemplify a Community of Professional Learners
(continued)

High Plains	Desert River	Low Country
Intentional Collective Learning		
The team members without hesitation shared the focus of their learning, why they were learning that, and how they were doing their collective learning.	The administrative team made the decision about professional learning to prepare staff for their new roles. However, the department teams continued their focused learning and working together, particularly as their turn to create the lessons came up, with the reading specialist available to them for assistance with their learning.	As they examined student work together and compared evidence of student learning to the state standards, all teachers reached an "a-ha" moment at one time or another and incorporated that new learning into their teaching.
Relational Conditions		
The 1st-grade team members had worked together for several years, and had learned to share openly with their colleagues about their instructional skills, whether of high quality or low. They had developed skills to address conflict, and "had developed a great deal of trust in one another." These factors and their commitment to serving their students well contributed to their pleasant and very productive relations with one another.	Although the new program and role for the staff members was "given" to them, they were concerned about their students and were grateful for this resolution for their students' benefit–after some introductory time. They had been in the same school for some years, had been to potluck suppers, weddings, and funerals as the years passed. Their basic knowledge of and respect for one another contributed to their willingness to begin the new experience of working together in a subject area for which they were not certified–a signal that suggests stronger relationships, including trust, can develop.	The level of trust and respect that the principal gave to the teachers, along with the value teachers found in their professional learning teams, removed barriers from teachers' ability to share their strengths and weaknesses openly and honestly. It was captured in one teacher's statement, "My teammates have my back."

Table 9.1. How the Schools Exemplify a Community of Professional Learners
(continued)

High Plains	Desert River	Low Country
Peers' Shared Practices		
As the team moved into transferring their learning about the new writing program to their classrooms, they initiated (at the principal's suggestion) visiting one another's classrooms to observe the host teacher, scripting observations of the teacher and meeting later in the day to share, discuss, and plan for revisions of the lesson. In this way, the visiting teacher as well as the host teacher learned more about transferring what they had learned in their PLC to the classroom.	The department teams, early in their creation of lessons and using the lessons of other departments, were not ready to host visitors from other teams in their classrooms while they were teaching the reading lessons. They were, however, just entertaining the idea of inviting their teammates to observe them and to give feedback related to the observations—this was to come very soon, as they were becoming comfortable in their new role as reading teachers.	The teachers moved beyond sharing tips, tricks, and techniques and opened themselves to sharing lessons, developing common assessments, analyzing the results, adjusting the assessments when they were found lacking and adjusting their instruction, and again, sharing the results of the adjustments. Deep sharing and collective learning had become the norm.

decision-making. Developing these skills makes it possible for the teachers to determine where they need to focus their own learning attention in order to become more effective in producing improved student results. In turn, their determination of improved student outcomes results easily in their creating, for their students, a vision of success, which will guide their own learning and that of the students. In this school, the principal plays a significant role in providing teachers with the opportunities for their group study and articulation of a vision of improvement for their students.

Such a public focus on teachers' classroom practice is not well developed in Desert River School, where teachers have lived together for some years but have not initially developed the sophistication for independent problem solving. Thus, the principal, with his administrative team, provides them with a program and a vision of what they will do to undertake the challenge of improving adolescent reading for their students. It would appear that, with the help of the reading specialist, the administrators and teachers will gain new knowledge and skills about a vision for, and delivery of, a program for students' reading improvement.

In Low Country, district-level leaders were introduced and tutored in the Professional Teaching and Learning Cycle (PTLC). The superintendent was an instructionally oriented one, and keen about professional development. When he learned about PTLC, he was immediately interested, and arranged for district leaders to learn about this process. The school already had an established time for teachers to meet, and the teaching staff members were trained in the use of data. The vision of what the professional learning community would be doing in its meetings was articulated: looking at student learning expectations, researching best practices in order to teach for those expectations, and holding one another accountable for their students' learning results.

Shared leadership. As noted in the commentary about the three schools' visioning process, the principal in High Plains has developed the personal and professional comfort level, as well as the skills of the staff, to give latitude to the teams to pursue the learning needs of their students as well as their own, and to articulate a vision and plan for doing so. They have gained the skills for taking these leadership roles as a result of several years of effort on the part of the principal, who shares leadership with the staff, as well as supporting its development.

To address a significant student achievement issue, the positional leadership of Desert River School moves abruptly to solve the problem. Although this move gains attention and participation by the teaching staff, it does not provide opportunities for the staff to engage in guided problem investigation and exploration of solutions. It would appear that the principal will endorse the departments' work in contributing to the resolution of the reading problem, and will possibly allow decision-making and authority distribution within the department teams. Whether any planned and guided efforts will be advanced for developing and sharing leadership is not evident at this time.

Leadership at the district level, as noted, initiated and led school leaders, coaches, and others at Low Country Middle School in the steps and strategies of their intended PLC work. This leadership was direct and strong in its initial period, but very soon, the teachers themselves in their community conversations were facilitating the meetings where members were raising questions, examining curriculum in which one teacher noted the lack of material to teach a stated standard. This stimulated all the grade-level teachers to search for other omissions. This led to deeper conversations about how to reorganize specific units so they would make more sense than they did in their presentation in textbooks. The teachers were off and running, taking charge of content and instructional strategies. It became clear that distributed leadership was the *modus operandi*.

Structural conditions. At High Plains, it seems that the logistical and physical conditions necessary for the grade-level teams to meet and work are in place: time, location, material and human resources, and communication with the principal. Likewise, at Desert River, these same resources have been provided to all the departments. In addition, an instructional coach, the reading specialist, is on board to respond to any needs of the staff about the new reading approach. At Low Country, the district-level administrators had been charged with making certain that the schools had the time, place, and resources needed, including instructional coaches and external consultants, when needed. As a result of district-level direction, coaches met with the communities, and the principals and/or assistant principals were expected to attend also. Making clear that the schools would conduct their learning communities with administrators and coaches present (with their frequency also defined) added a structural element that contributed to the success of Low Country School.

Becoming a PLC

The three dimensions, above, provided the strategic and structural framework for initiating the PLC. Now comes the harder substantive and conceptual work of the community and the three dimensions that will support this challenging work.

Intentional collective learning. With their experience in teamwork and their focus on students, the High Plains team is running with "the bit in their mouth" in creating and executing plans for the learning that they will need in order to deliver the writing program for students' learning. They have given useful thinking about short- and long-range plans that reveal what to do and how to do the learning to which they have committed. This work is familiar to them and they go about it efficiently.

At Desert River, the administrative team has used its authority to adopt a reading approach for the teachers and to provide the professional learning for them, as the entire staff engages in the implementation of the program. As the department teams become familiar with the organization and arrangements of the program, and as they gain expertise in the creation of their portion of the program, they will employ learning for themselves in order to do the creating. In this group learning by the department members, they are clearly engaging in intentional collective learning. It will be interesting to ascertain if and how this group learning, focused on a topic of their choice, extrapolates beyond this program.

A protocol that directed the conversations for the Low Country School soon was replaced by the teachers' close examination of their curriculum and how their students were faring in its use. The teachers' keen scrutiny and thoughtful reflections about their findings were key to the actions that they determined to take, to look into various concepts and strategies that were "handed down to them" but which they found contained errors or were incomplete. In their review of their work and that of their students, they focused attention on the needs of students and targeted their own learning, first, in order to prepare to deliver a higher-quality instructional program for students. They took charge of their own learning through the lens of their students' unsatisfactory performance.

Relational conditions. There is a history of continuity for the members of the High Plains 1st-grade team. They have been together in their grade-level assignment for some years, and know one another well. They have shared celebrations and disagreements, developing a means for resolving conflict, which they have learned will happen along the way, of close and candid working and learning together. They have learned that they can count on their colleagues to do what they promise to do, and in this and other ways trust has developed among the members. They share a strong commitment to their students' learning and this factor drives their work and relationships.

Although Desert River staff members worked alongside one another for some years, their working arrangements never dictated that they work in teams, together resolving instructional issues or other matters. When the new reading approach brought them into intimate working proximity, some time was required for them to adjust to this new arrangement of depending on one another, for creating instructional plans that would be publicized and used by the entire faculty—what a challenge!

Understanding their concerns and initial discomfort, the principal demonstrated his commitment by taking on the same tasks and challenges as the teachers. He further realized that staff members would require considerable professional learning to be able to execute the new approach successfully for their students. Providing the assistance of a coach for any staff members' needs was further evidence of his attending to the staff's feelings and reactions. But it takes time to develop positive regard for colleagues with whom one has not previously been engaged. As the staff learns the new approach and becomes more comfortable with it and their department mates, acceptance and trust have the clear possibility of developing. This will require time and cannot be rushed, but the principal and his team are giving the staff a great deal of support that will encourage mutual respect, appreciation of department colleagues' work, and trust in one another.

At Low Country, teachers have benefited immeasurably from the principal, who gave them his respect and trust in their capacities. Teachers found these identical qualities in one another as they developed into a mature community of questioners and learners, with their focus on their students' needs. Sharing their strengths and shortcomings is clearly an indicator of the strong trusting relationship that they place in one another.

Peers' shared practices. The rather formal practice of teachers inviting their peers into their classrooms to observe them at work and to give feedback is not for the faint of heart, and is the last of the six components to develop in most schools. The reporting of classroom activities that teachers do in the workroom or teacher's lounge, or at the lunchroom table, is an informal means of sharing expertise, activities that others might use in their classroom. By no means does it include feedback on any individuals who might choose to try the newly learned activities, shared in the lounge.

The 1st-grade team at High Plains uses both procedures: 1) "sharing expertise," or teachers telling one another about some activities that occurred in their classrooms; and 2) visiting one another in their classrooms to more formally observe and provide feedback to the host teacher in order to gain new and improved ways of teaching that will benefit their students. They are early into their arrangements to visit one another's classrooms to observe and give useful feedback. Their lack of reluctance to engage in the visits to observe peers and to engage in the challenging task of providing feedback suggests that they are comfortable with one another and with their teaching prowess, although they are always looking to improve their classroom practice and for alternative ways of delivering effective instruction.

Staff members in the Desert River departments are not yet ready to expose themselves to their colleagues in other departments, although they are thinking of doing so with their own department members. This will be a major step for these teachers, and understandably so, as they are early in their development of team or community work. With the continued support of their principal and the reading specialist, and given the time for developing the knowledge and skills demanded of the reading project, they, too, can develop comfort and learn to value this means of improving their work for students.

Members of the Low Country learning communities engaged in deep sharing, open feedback, and collective learning. These activities were conducted in the transparent and porous atmosphere and norms of the communities. Their meetings were characterized by their open and candid conversations, and by their consistent focus on students. They have not yet become involved in the formal visitation of classrooms to observe and provide feedback. It would not be surprising to learn that they will do so in the immediate future.

It is not difficult to discern the degree to which each of these schools' staff members reflect the six attributes of a community of professional learners. But what impact does this have on the educators' professionalism? That is the next question of interest.

THE EFFECTS OF COMMUNITY WORK ON PROFESSIONALISM

Out of the various traits and characteristics related to being a professional, we have suggested that there are two categories that most immediately warrant our attention for increasing the professionalism of educators:

- Engagement in a formal preparation and certification process that meets standards set by the profession itself, and
- Possession of a professional orientation exemplified by a commitment to the continuous acquisition of the professional learning and delivery of the actions needed to support the best interests of those served by the profession (Chapter 1).

Formal Preparation and Certification

Although there are some teachers who are hired short of appropriate certification due to urgent local needs, for the most part, educators have a sheepskin in hand and a license to perform in schools at the level and in the academic area of their certification. However, the unfortunate truth is that many of our universities and colleges that prepare teachers are themselves in dire need of reform. Another factor for consideration is that, in our schools currently, there is a very different student population from that of previous years.

In our classrooms, in many urban areas especially, there are multiple languages brought by students who represent a wide variety of family backgrounds, cultures, and heritages; socioeconomic status; and other descriptors. The teacher, who has been inadequately prepared for this diversity, faces enormous challenges.

Further, leaders in education and in the corporate sector are demanding student results in skills such as critical thinking, problem solving, serving as cooperative team players, becoming creative producers, demonstrating clear communication, and others. These skills will better prepare them to succeed as a contributing citizen in a global economy. Such characteristics are far different from what we have included in K–12 curriculum guides in the past. And currently our classroom teachers are not being well prepared to develop these 21st-century skills in our students.

It is clear that teacher preparation and continuous development cannot cease at the end of the bachelor's or master's degree if we are to have professional educators in our schools. Rather, professional development must become a significant part of the workplace. It is essential to provide opportunities for continuous learning, so that, as Learning Forward (the recently changed name of the National Staff Development Council) has declared:

> Every educator engages in effective professional learning every day so every student achieves.

The professional learning community setting provides the environment for this professional learning to happen continuously and seamlessly. The bottom-line purpose of the PLC is the *learning* of the professionals, learning that is tightly connected to the learning needs of their students. The PLC is the most powerful structure/strategy available for the required, continuous, formal, and informal learning of the education force. We see this in action in several components of the effective PLC.

Shared vision of improvement. In this component, teachers and principals, who are professionally oriented, specify the goal(s) of their intended learning in explicit terms, providing them with a map toward learning that will improve their preparation for delivering effective instruction for students. All too frequently in the past, the anticipated learning has been poorly articulated, is shabby in its specificity, and provides poor guidance for the professional learners.

Intentional collective learning. Collective learning (in a group setting) promotes richer and deeper learning outcomes. This learning in the PLC is identified from the professionals' reviews of student performance data, whose results direct the professionals' collective learning. The professionals intentionally focus on the new knowledge and skills that will enable them to become more effective in producing desired student outcomes.

Peers' shared practice. This additional avenue for new learning confirms and/or leads to revisions of teaching practice. Thus, professionals use it to improve their individual practice as well as improve the practice of the entire school staff. In this way, professional peers provide specific support for one another, and hold one another accountable for student learning as they engage in their identified adult learning needs for the school.

High Plains School's 1st-grade team can most assuredly be considered a professional learning community, and reflects a strong professional identity with self-directed learning. As High Plains' description indicates, the 1st-grade teachers are active in the components noted above, continuously assessing their effectiveness, engaging in deep and thoughtful study of their students' performance data, and determining where they need to give attention to their adult learning. Desert River School's staff has not yet developed the professional initiative to address their own learning, and still wait for their administrators to give them direction. At Low Country School, the PLC members have assumed the responsibility for the accuracy, authenticity, and completeness of the curriculum that they will use in order to ensure that students achieve the expected standards for their grade level. Further, in a group format, they invite one another to assess their teaching through examination of students' work and to give feedback in an open and constructive way. How the personnel of these three schools operate in making certain that they have the preparation necessary for their job (through their self-directed learning, filling the gap left from their formal training) separates them distinctly. High Plains and Low Country engage in self-imposed continuous professional learning directed by their students' success, or lack of success, while Desert River personnel, based on these criteria, in their present condition, are denied the label of true professionals.

A Professional Orientation

The abstract term *professional orientation* can best be understood and is exemplified by individuals who are committed to the best interests of those whom they serve; in education, those individuals are the students. Let us examine how this plays out in the three schools' PLCs.

Shared vision of improvement. It has been noted that the shared vision component of PLC members focuses relentlessly on students and how to benefit them. This surely connects with working in "the best interests of those whom they serve," the students. Each of the schools' stories depicts staff members working for the benefit of their constituents—the students and their students' learning. This commitment to clients adds another dimension to the professionalism of High Plains, to Desert River, and to Low Country staff, although this commitment appears more mature at High Plains and Low Country.

Intentional collective learning. Participating in collective learning that is intentional and based on their students' needs is a strong component at High Plains and at Low Country. The PLC members at these two schools, who exhibit a high degree of professionalism, have learned how to read, study, understand, and interpret data so that they are able to use it for decision-making, done in the best interests of their students. The adults here are not learning about the latest new educational fad, unless it contributes to their ability to serve their students more effectively. Their learning is sharply focused and intentionally directed to what they need to learn in order to teach their students, so that student performance improves—they direct their commitments to their clients, exhibiting a professional orientation that directs their behaviors.

Staff members at Desert River are in an early developmental stage in collective learning, engaging in the learning so as to create the lessons that they are obligated to do. When they themselves begin to identify and to initiate their learning (based on their students' performance needs) and act consistently upon it, they will more fully reflect the professional orientation of the true professional.

Peers' shared practices. Coupled with the intentional learning that the community does are the follow-up activities of the professionals as they share practices when using the new learning in the classroom. When done well, this observation and its feedback can be very supportive, and enhances implementation of the new knowledge and skills that have been developed in the community's intentional learning. Inviting peers into the classroom to observe and then conduct a feedback session is also another opportunity to learn more deeply, and to gain additional competency for transferring the learning from the community setting into classroom practice. However, this set of activities requires a great deal of trust between and among the members, as well as multiple opportunities to execute and practice the activities before the community's professional members become comfortable.

High Plains is in the early stages of peer observation and feedback, suggested by the principal. As teachers gain competence and confidence with these processes, they will engage in additional peer coaching, leading to improved implementation of their PLC learning. These professional interactions contribute to their patina of professional orientation. Desert River is in an infancy stage—perhaps more accurately, in the pre-birth stage, as it has some poorly articulated plans with this PLC component (as noted earlier, this component is almost always the last to develop in the PLC). When the PLC members develop the comfort and skills to make these classroom visits and offer feedback, they will, in fact, be supporting their colleagues but also monitoring classroom practice, a very high-level professional behavior. Wisely, they are considering this activity, but it is yet to be developed.

Structural conditions. Providing the logistical/structural requirements that support their meetings has been addressed in these three schools. In other schools where this component is not readily available, educators will not let this lack of readiness stand in their way, but will find the resources in order to undertake the PLC work. Working in the effectively organized PLC provides the time and place, the platform for the participation of individuals and their development of a professional orientation, reflecting the behaviors recognized in professionals.

Relational conditions. Relationships! Relationships! This requirement for the productive operation of a PLC is the basis for the success of any cooperative or collegial enterprise. The PLC thrives on the high regard and respect that members hold for one another, which develops over time as the members interact. But this activity requires a great deal of trust, a very mature level of trust that each member demonstrates for the others. Having lived with and collaborated with their members for several years, the High Plains team has "slugged" through countless meetings where differences were expressed and resolved. They understand now that to express differences adds to the richness of their discussions and the possibilities for new ways of teaching for student learning. They have accepting and positive attitudes toward their teammates and toward the ideas, skills, and knowledge that each person brings. In short, they rely on one another and share both trust in one another and individual trustworthiness as a common trait. This foundation makes it possible to be exceptionally productive in researching new ways of teaching, making plans to use the new way, learning about using it together, and implementing it in their classrooms in order to benefit students—a visible descriptor of their ever-growing professionalism.

Although Desert River staff members have known one another for several years, they have not had the opportunity or occasion to work together intimately to study data, explore solutions to address students' unacceptable performance, make plans, cuss and discuss ideas and possibilities, coming to agreements productively. To become a vitally functioning PLC, they will develop these skills and predispositions, which could pave the way for them to increase their professional orientation in the future.

Low Country personnel have benefited from the futuristic vision and planning of their district leaders and the campus administrators. This has provided a sheltered environment in which the PLC has been planned for, provided for, encouraged, monitored, and assisted through its stages of development. The members have reached a high state of PLC maturity. Their self-initiated, deep, and thoroughgoing exploration of students' performance, and their attention given to their own learning in order to implement new teaching practices that will benefit students, expresses a strong professional orientation. These educators "stand tall" in the respect and admiration they command from their colleagues, and parents as well.

Shared leadership. The active element of shared leadership may well be the most important ingredient and the imperative for the development of a professional orientation and subsequent professional behaviors of the teacher-members of the PLC. The PLC is a self-organizing entity, determining its operational norms and distributing leadership through shared authority and decision-making, as noted in the shared leadership component description. In this environment, the members of the PLC—whether teachers, administrators, or others—determine their self-initiated independent and collective activities. Shared leadership is demonstrated as the members make decisions about the what, why, and how of their intentional learning; this adult learning is always designed to benefit students.

It would not seem possible for the learning communities to design and take action if the positional leadership of the school does not provide this opportunity. It should be understood, however, that the grade-level teams or whole-school communities make decisions and take actions within a prescribed set of boundaries or parameters. They are not free to take unrestricted action. School and district policies and norms remain intact so that the PLC makes decisions within these frames. Nonetheless, there is ample space for PLC decision-making and actions designed by the members. It is this freedom that makes it possible for the members to generate ideas, materials, strategies, and the means whereby to assess their actions and products. In turn, this environment makes it possible for the PLC members to develop a professional orientation, followed by the behaviors of a true professional.

In a study that relates leadership orientation to teacher professionalism, Tschannen-Moran makes the following observation:

> The evidence suggests that for schools to meet the calls to function as professional learning communities, attention needs to be paid to the ways that schools are managed. In schools that were managed with a professional orientation, as

evidenced by a less bureaucratic and authoritarian leadership style on the part of principals, teachers reported greater professionalism in the behavior of their colleagues. Faculty's perceptions of a flexible administrative orientation that facilitated, rather than hampered, their efforts correlated strongly with their perceptions that teachers were more likely to take their work seriously, demonstrate a high level of commitment, and go beyond minimum expectations to meet the needs of students. In these schools, teachers respected their colleagues' competence and expertise and reported that they were clearly engaged in the teaching process. Teachers worked cooperatively with one another and were enthusiastic about their work. Conversely, in schools with a bureaucratic, rule-bound orientation, teachers were less likely to conduct themselves as professionals and to go beyond minimum expectations with students. (2009, p. 239)

Sharing and self-initiating action characterizes the PLC of High Plains and of Low Country, suggesting groups of professionals who do not wait to be told what to do, but move to determine action. They have several years of experience to know how to operate for the design and declaration of action. These teams exemplify a professional orientation and professional behaviors. Desert River may reach this level, but it will require time and leadership. This leadership will be shared and given to the staff by the administration, along with administrators' support in developing the staff as leaders.

RUMINATIONS AND REFLECTIONS

Several additional ideas have appeared as we have pursued the concept of professionalism or a professional orientation, and these deserve some consideration.

The System

Although the actions of the school administrator, the principal, are of unique importance, as noted above, there is an additional factor that impacts the developmental possibilities of the PLC's attributes, and consequently, the members' learning and growth to become professionally oriented. This factor is the system, its organizational policies and/or culture, and, particularly, decision-making practices.

We have had the opportunity to work alongside superintendents in several school districts (the sizes ranged from nine to 12 schools). These superintendents made clear the expectations that the schools and their sub-parts (grade-level teams, academic departments, and so on) would organize professional learning communities–for the purpose of continuous learning of the staff. They did not dictate how the PLCs would be organized, when they would meet (although we know of districts that have managed the entire district schedule so that students depart early on one afternoon during the week, making it possible for the whole staff or parts of it to meet), or where the communities would meet.

Most of these district leaders initiated their PLC projects with sharing student achievement data from statewide testing, urging the schools to add other sources of student performance results. To support the study, interpretation, and use of these data, the district office staff provided intense professional development for supporting the school staffs in their "learning about data" sessions. It is important to note that several of the "supers" attended the data study at the schools where the sessions were scheduled. They operated in these sessions as any learner, sleeves rolled up, participating in the activities, with cell phones turned off. They required no airtime exceeding that of the other learners.

This is one example of superintendents' support of the PLC effort and their attention to its needs. Their attention did not cease after data study, but continued throughout the first 2 years of the development period of PLCs by monitoring the efforts at the schools: showing up at a PLC meeting occasionally, asking the principals for progress reports (which required the principals to monitor and give attention to nurturing the PLCs), requesting that school teams periodically report their activities to the school board at their meetings. One of the school systems created a monitoring and reporting scheme whereby the principal of each school gathered information about the PLCs in that school;

> Principals shared their reports with various district office staff (who
>   would occasionally visit the PLC meetings);
> District office staff gathered to make a bimonthly report to the
>   superintendent.

This process encouraged all staff at the classroom level, campus administrator level, and district office to give attention, become informed, and serve in monitoring action. Such activities emerging from district office contributed greatly to the scale-up process of PLC development and implementation.

These superintendents provided a great deal of opportunity for the school communities to engage in their own decision-making about their norms, how to organize, and how they would go about doing the learning that was expected to be related to the needs of the students—needs gleaned from the data study. Several of these superintendents themselves were engaged with other superintendents in learning communities, and reported to their principals about their activities in their role-alike communities, encouraging principals to form learning groups also.

One of the superintendents made very clear his expectations through modeling. At the district office or on school campuses, he always had a book under his arm. He would stop teachers to share something that he had just read, or to ask a teacher about some idea that appeared in the book. If the book were at the student level (even for 2nd-graders), he could be found chatting with two or three students, referring to the book, to engage them in conversation about the book's ideas or lessons. In all conversations, he referenced learning—with students, staff, and parents.

In school systems such as these, unit managers (department heads, grade-level chairs, or principals of the school) allow for and encourage the staff's independent thinking and shared decision-making, promoting such norms and policies. Where power, authority, and decision-making are not shared and supported, it becomes challenging in the extreme for the individuals in that community setting to make much progress toward developing professional orientation, professional attitudes or perspectives, or increasing professional expertise.

Both High Plains and Low Country schools have district leadership and policies that supported their initiation and their development as professional learning communities. This has enabled them to move more efficiently to maturity as PLCs. Desert River was in a district that talked about PLC development, but gave modest attention and support for it. Thus, this school has been late in moving in that direction.

Membership in a Profession

Does being a member of a profession guarantee that the members act with a professional orientation? The answer is "Apparently not, or there would not be suits against doctors for malpractice or to disbar lawyers." Being a member and acting or behaving as a true professional are not one and the same. Returning to the defining characteristics of a professional:

- Being certified, having the knowledge and skills necessary to meet the needs of clients, and
- Having a strong sense of calling and a *commitment* to serving clients ...

It would seem that the term *commitment* is key to the actions or behaviors of the true professional. An individual can possess the knowledge and skills and never engage them for the benefit of others. Equally important, the individual can have "a strong sense of calling," but no satisfactory knowledge and skills, and never take effective action in serving others.

We believe the pathway from a professional learning community to becoming a truly *professional* educator is a twisting and turning one, with obvious holes in the road and some substantial boulders as well. But we also believe the obstacles can be challenges that allow for solutions. For example, time is required, not only for the weekly meeting of the PLC–2 to 3 years of concentrated effort are needed to achieve full efficiency, effectiveness, and collective efficacy, although, as seen in the examples, great strides can be made in the early stages.

The professional learning community is basically a classroom, school, and district improvement strategy. Like all improvement efforts, professional learning is required for a successful journey. Although the PLC setting is especially powerful for individuals' continuous learning and contributions to their effectiveness, the presence of true educational professionals at the helm and in the chart room will be necessary for guiding and maintaining a school's continued success in providing quality teaching and challenging opportunities for its students' learning accomplishments. Additionally, participation in a professional learning community where teachers continually acquire new professional knowledge and skills, trust one another, and are open to learning together helps communicate to those outside of the classroom that teachers are professionals who deserve the respect that comes with such a critical job.

The words of William Glasser seem to be a fitting summary of our message to educators about taking the high road on the pathway to professionalism:

> If you want to change attitudes, start with a change in behavior. In other words, begin to act the part, as well as you can, of the person you would rather be, the person you most want to become.

References

Alkin, M. C. (1992). Professional development of teachers. *Encyclopedia of Educational Research* (6th ed., Vol. 3, pp. 1045–1052). New York: Macmillan.

Bandura, A. (1993). Perceived self-efficacy in cognitive development and functioning. *Educational Psychologist, 28*(2), 117–148.

Barth, R. (1990). *Improving schools from within: Teachers, parents, and principals can make the difference.* San Francisco: Jossey-Bass.

Barth, R. (2004). *Learning by heart.* San Francisco: Jossey-Bass.

Barth, R. (2006). Improving relationships within the schoolhouse. *Educational Leadership, 63*(6), 8–13.

Berry, B., et al. (2011). *Teaching 2030: What we must do for our students and our public schools–now and in the future.* New York: Teachers College Press.

Bobbett, J. J., Ellett, C. D., Teddlie, C., Olivier, D. F., & Rugutt, J. (2002, April). School culture and school effectiveness in demonstrably effective and ineffective schools. Paper presented at the annual meeting of the American Education Research Association, New Orleans.

Boyd, V., & Hord, S. M. (1994, April). Principals and the new paradigm: Schools as learning communities. Paper presented at the annual meeting of the American Educational Research Association, New Orleans.

Bryk, A., & Schneider, B. (2002). *Trust in schools: A core resource for improvement.* New York: Russell Sage.

Bulger, P. (1972). *Education as a profession.* Washington, DC: ERIC Clearinghouse on Teacher Education

Burbules, N., & Densmore, K. (1991). The limits of making teaching a profession. *Educational Policy, 5*(1), 44–63.

Darling-Hammond, L. (1988). Policy and professionalism. In A. Lieberman (Ed.), *Building a professional culture in schools* (pp. 55–77). New York: Teachers College Press.

Darling-Hammond, L., & Sykes, G. (2003). Wanted: A national teacher supply policy for education: The right way to meet the "Highly Qualified Teacher" challenge. *Education Policy Analysis Archives, 11*(33). Retrieved from http://epaa.asu.edu/epaa/v11n33/

Darling-Hammond, L., Wei, R., Andree, A., Richardson, N., & Orphanos, S. (2009). *Professional learning in the learning profession: A status report on teacher development in the United States and abroad.* Oxford, OH: National Staff Development Council.

Donovan, S. (2009, February 11). Building "institutional infrastructure" and bringing research into the classroom. *Education Week, 28*(21), 24–25.

Edmonds, R. (1979). Effective schools for the urban poor. *Educational Leadership,* *37*(2), 15–23.

Ermeling, B. A. (2010). Tracing the effects of teacher inquiry on classroom practice. *Teaching and Teacher Education, 26,* 377–388.

Etzioni, A. (1969). *The semi-professions and their organisation: Teachers, nurses and social workers.* New York: Free Press.

Gallimore, R., & Ermeling, B. A. (2010, April 14). Five keys to effective teacher learning teams. *Education Week, 29*(29).

Gallimore, R., Ermeling, B. A., Saunders, W. M., & Goldenberg, C. N. (2009). Moving the learning of teaching closer to practice: Teacher education implications of school-based inquiry teams. *The Elementary School Journal, 109*(5), 537–553.

Glazer, J. (2008). Educational professionalism: An inside-out view. *American Journal of Education, 114*(2), 169–189.

Gleick, J. (1987). *Chaos: Making a new science.* London: Cardinal.

Goddard, R. D., Hoy, W. K., & Woolfolk Hoy, A. (2000). Collective teacher efficacy: Its meaning, measure, and impact on student achievement. *American Educational Research Journal, 37*(2), 479–507.

Goldhaber, D., & Hannaway, J. (Eds.). (2009). *Creating a new teaching profession.* Washington, DC: Urban Institute Press.

Gonzalez, C. E., Resta, P. E., & De Hoyos, M. L. (2005, April). Barriers and facilitators on implementation of policy initiatives to transform higher education teaching-learning process. Paper presented at the annual meeting of the American Educational Research Association, Montreal.

Hall, G. E., & Hord, S. M. (2011). *Implementing change: Patterns, principles, and potholes* (3rd Ed.). Boston: Allyn & Bacon.

Hipp, K. K., & Huffman, J. B. (Eds.). (2010). *Demystifying professional learning communities: School leadership at its best.* New York: Rowman & Littlefield.

Hirsh, S. A., & Hord, S. M. (2008). Role of professional learning in advancing quality teaching and student learning. *21st century education: A reference handbook* (Vol. 2). Thousand Oaks, CA: Sage.

Hord, S. M. (Ed.). (2004). *Learning together, leading together: Changing schools through professional learning communities.* New York: Teachers College Press.

Hord, S. M., & Hirsh, S. A. (2008). Making the promise a reality. In A. M. Blankstein, P. D. Houston, & R. W. Cole (Eds.), *Sustaining professional learning communities* (pp. 23–40). Thousand Oaks, CA: Corwin Press.

Hord, S. M., & Sommers, W. A. (2008). *Leading professional learning communities: Voices from research and practice.* Thousand Oaks, CA: Corwin.

Hord, S. M., Stiegelbauer, S. M., Hall, G. E., & George, A. A. (2006). *Measuring implementation in schools: Innovation configurations.* Austin, TX: Southwest Educational Development Laboratory.

Joyce, B., & Showers, B. (2002). *Student achievement through staff development.* Alexandria, VA: Association for Supervision and Curriculum Development.

Kegan, R., & Lahey, L. (2001). *How the way we talk can change the way we work: Seven languages for transformation.* San Francisco: Jossey-Bass.

Klein, J. (2011, March 7). As goes Wisconsin . . . So goes the nation. *Time, 177*(9). Retrieved from http://www.time.com/time/magazine/article/0,9171,2055203,00.html

Larson, M. S. (1977). *The rise of professionalism: A sociological analysis.* Berkeley: University of California Press.

Lee, V. E., Smith, J. B., & Croninger, R. G. (1995, Fall). Another look at high school restructuring. *Issues in restructuring schools.* Madison: Center on Organization and Restructuring of Schools, School of Education, University of Wisconsin at Madison.

Lieberman, M. (1997). *The teacher unions: How the NEA and AFT sabotage reform and hold students, parents, teachers, and taxpayers hostage to bureaucracy.* New York: The Free Press.

Little, J. W. (1982). Norms of collegiality and experimentation: Workplace conditions of school success. *American Educational Research Journal, 19*(3), 325–340.

Little, J. W. (2006). *Professional development and professional community in the learning-centered school.* Arlington, VA: National Education Association.

Lortie, D. (1975). *Schoolteacher.* Chicago: University of Chicago Press.

Louis, K. S., Kruse, S. D., & Associates. (1995). *Professionalism and community: Perspectives on reforming urban schools.* Thousand Oaks, CA: Corwin Press.

Monaghan, E. J. (March, 1988). Literacy instruction and gender in colonial New England. *American Quarterly, 40,* 18–41.

McLaughlin, M. W., & Talbert, J. E. (1993). *Contexts that matter for teaching and learning.* Stanford: Center for Research on the Context of Secondary School Teaching, Stanford University.

McMahon, L. G. (2003). Rekindling the spirit to teach: A qualitative study of the personal and professional renewal of teachers. Unpublished doctoral dissertation, Gonzaga University, Spokane, WA.

National Commission on Teaching and America's Future. (1996). *What matters most: Teaching for America's future.* New York: Author.

National Commission on Teaching and America's Future. (2007). *The high cost of teacher turnover* [Policy Brief]. Retrieved from http://www.nctaf.org

National Commission on Teaching and America's Future. (2010). *Who will teach? Experience matters* [Research Report]. Retrieved from http://www.nctaf.org

National Council for Accreditation of Teacher Education. (2010). *Transforming teacher education through clinical practice: A national strategy to prepare effective teachers.* Washington, DC: Author.

National Staff Development Council. (2001). *Standards for staff development, revised.* Oxford, OH: Author.

Neil, R. (1986). Eleven traditional methods of inservice teacher education. (ERIC Document Reproduction Service No. ED 200 244 SP 030 624).

Newmann, F., & Wehlage, G. (1997). *Successful school restructuring: A report to the public and educators by the Center on Organization and Restructuring of Schools.* Madison, WI: Document Service, Wisconsin Center for Education Research.

Paige, R. (2007). *The war against hope: How teachers' unions hurt children, hinder teachers, and endanger public education.* Nashville, TN: Nelson Current.

Palmer, P. (2004). *A hidden wholeness: The journey toward an undivided life.* San Francisco: Jossey-Bass.

Palmer, P. (2007). *The courage to teach: Exploring the inner landscape of a teacher's life.* San Francisco: Jossey-Bass.

Pfeffer, J., & Sutton, R. (2000). *The knowing-doing gap: How smart companies turn knowledge into action.* Boston: Harvard Business School Publishing.

Podgursky, M. (2004). Improving academic performance in U.S. public schools: Why teacher licensing is (almost) irrelevant. In F. Hess, A. Rotherham, & K. Walsh (Eds.), *A qualified teacher in every classroom: Appraising old answers and new ideas* (pp. 255–277). Cambridge, MA: Harvard Education Press.

Postman, N., & Weingartner, C. (1969). *Teaching as a subversive activity.* New York: Dell.

Poutiatine, M. I. (2005). The role of identity and integrity in teacher development: Towards a grounded theory of teacher formation. Unpublished doctoral dissertation, Gonzaga University, Spokane, WA.

Ravitch, D. (2010a). *The life and death of the great American school system: How testing and choice are undermining education.* Philadelphia: Basic Books.

Ravitch, D. (2010b, November 11). The myth of charter schools. *New York Review of Books.*

Rosenholtz, S. J. (1989). *Teachers' workplace: The social organizations of schools.* New York: Longman.

Roy, P., & Hord, S. (2003). *Moving NSDC's staff development standards into practice: Innovation configurations.* Oxford, OH: National Staff Development Council.

Sarason, S. B. (1993). *The predictable failure of educational reform.* New York: Jossey-Bass.

Saunders, W. M., Goldenberg, C. N., & Gallimore, R. (2009). Increasing achievement by focusing grade-level teams on improving classroom learning: A prospective, quasi-experimental study of Title I Schools. *American Educational Research Journal, 46*(4), 1006–1033.

Schmoker, M. (2003). Planning for failure? *Education Week, 22*(22), 39.

SEDL. (2008). *The professional teaching and learning cycle: Introduction.* Austin, TX: Author.

Senge, P. (1990). *The fifth discipline.* New York: Doubleday Current.

Shulman, L. (2004). *The wisdom of practice: Essays on teaching, learning and learning to teach.* San Francisco: Jossey-Bass.

Sugg, R. S. (1978). *Motherteacher: The feminization of American education.* Charlottesville: University Press of Virginia.

Taylor, G., & Runte, R. (Eds.). (1995). *Thinking about teaching: An introduction.* Toronto: Harcourt Brace.

Tobia, E. (2007). The professional teaching and learning cycle: Implementing a standards-based approach to professional development. *SEDL Letter, 19*(1), 11–15.

Tschannen-Moran, M. (2004). *Trust matters: Leadership for successful schools.* San Francisco: Jossey-Bass.

Tschannen-Moran, M. (2009). Fostering teacher professionalism in schools: The role of leadership orientation and trust. *Educational Administration Quarterly, 45*(2), 217–247.

Vescio, V., Ross, D., & Adams, A. (2008). A review of research on the impact of professional learning communities on teaching practice and student learning. *Teaching and Teacher Education, 24,* 80–91.

Wheatley, M. (2006). *Leadership and the new science: Discovering order in a chaotic world.* San Francisco: Berrett-Koehler.

Zouyu, Z. (2002). The teaching profession: To be or to do? *Journal of Education for Teaching, 28*(3), 211–215.

Index

About the Authors

Shirley M. Hord (Ph.D., Boerne, TX, shirley.hord@learningforward.org) is Scholar Laureate, in association with Learning Forward (previously named the National Staff Development Council), following her retirement as the first Scholar Emerita at the Southwest Educational Development Laboratory, Austin, Texas. Prior to this work, she served on the faculty in the College of Education, Science Education Center, University of Texas, Austin; she was engaged in research on school change and improvement for 10 years in the federally funded R&D Center for Teacher Education, University of Texas at Austin. She authors articles, chapters, and books on school-based professional development, leadership, school change and improvement, and professional learning communities. In addition to her work with Gene Hall on the third edition of *Implementing Change: Patterns, Principles, and Potholes* (2011); her current book publications include *Learning Together, Leading Together: Changing Schools Through Professional Learning Communities* (Teachers College Press, 2004, with Patricia Roy); *Moving NSDC's Staff Development Standards Into Practice: Innovation Configurations* (National Staff Development Council, 2003); *Leading Professional Learning Communities: Voices from Research and Practice* (2008); and *Guiding Professional Learning Communities: Inspiration, Challenge, Surprise, and Meaning* (2010). She monitors the Leadership for Change Networks, supports applications of the Concerns-Based Adoption Model, and designs and delivers professional development focused on educational change, school improvement, and school leadership. In addition to working with educators at all levels across the United States, Canada, and Mexico, she makes presentations and consults in Asia, Europe, Australia, and Africa.

Edward F. Tobia (Ed.D., Austin, TX, ed.tobia@gmail.com) currently works at SEDL in the Improving School Performance unit. He has extensive background in school improvement processes, leadership development, and professional development. He has 26 years of experience in public education as an elementary teacher, middle school assistant principal, elementary principal, director of elementary curriculum, and director of professional development. His work at SEDL has included coordinating state support for the Comprehensive School Reform Demonstration Program, a 5-year project focusing on helping schools and districts work more systemically, and supporting states' implementation of the No Child Left Behind Act. He has been the project director for two multiyear projects to assist districts and schools in building the internal capacity of school and district leaders (including teacher leaders) to sustain a systemic improvement process and assist with the design and implementation of an ongoing teacher development process. As a certified *Courage to Teach* and *Courage to Lead* facilitator, he has conducted introductory and long-term retreats to renew, sustain, and inspire public school educators.